Qi Dao - Tibetan

Shamanic Qigong

The Art of Being in the Flow

Lama Somananda Tantrapa

Academy of Qi Dao

Revised edition. First published by AuthorHouse on 08/13/2007.

ISBN: 978-1-4343-2027-8

Library of Congress Control Number: 2007905688

Cover design and illustrations by Patrick Burke of www.patrickburke.com.

Printed in U.S.A.

What other Qigong experts say about
Qi Dao – Tibetan Shamanic Qigong

Lama Tantrapa opens new windows, doors, pictures and dimensions to peer through. His book is sound, organized, developmentally structured, and good-humored. I learned a lot from reading it, and became aware of subtleties, aspects and dimensions I had previously missed, or had not paid attention to.

- James MacRitchie, L.Ac., founder of the National Qigong (Chi Kung) Association
Author of *Chi Kung - Energy for Life*

The uniqueness of Lama Tantrapa's book is in its emphasis on the foundational principles of Qigong rather than on the details of a particular form. This book is definitely not another exercise book. It is a deep exploration into the nature of "Being" as revealed through movement and energy awareness. This book will help you focus on the process rather than the end results and build the foundation for understanding the importance of movement in shaping the way you are.

- Mark Johnson, founder of the National Qigong Association
Producer of *Tai Chi for Seniors*

Lama Tantrapa has shared his precious family tradition revealing the connection between the way you hold yourself and your culture of movement. It will stimulate you to reveal and manifest innate life dreams as you establish a new paradigm of consciousness for yourself. The most profound dream experiences happened to me after reading this book on more than one occasion. Many doors were opened to deeper and deeper layers of awareness and insight into the intricacies of my subconscious. I certainly hope you will delve into this wonderful book to find greater healing, peace and joy in your life.

- Shoshanna Katzman, M.S., L.Ac., Former President of the National Qigong Association
Author of *Qigong for Staying Young*

Lama Tantrapa goes straight to the essence of Qi Dao teachings – that self-realization is synonymous with being in the flow. This requires awakening to the realization that one's individual life path is inseparable with the flow of the universal life force. Lama Tantrapa is constantly inviting each of us to step into that flow of universal life. His book contains both timeless wisdom, and daily practice instructions to help you on your way. The illustrations are some of the finest in print!

- Bonnitta Roy, Former President of the National Qigong Association
Founding Editor of *The Journal of Qigong in America*

Lama Tantrapa's attention to detail and nuance is at its best when elucidating the distinction between "intention" and "attention." When these qualities are applied to the topic of Qigong, his distinction between "inner essence" and "doing forms" makes that alone worth reading this book. Don't miss this rare opportunity to share the sacred heritage of this fascinating Qi Dao lineage holder. His writing has been in the making for centuries!

- Bernard Seif, Ed.D., DNM, SMC, Psychologist, Doctor of Natural Medicine
Author of *Daytime Prayer*

As you experience the philosophy of Qi Dao you will notice that it takes a different approach than classical Qigong. Its movements are not part of a structured form, thus allowing for greater freedom of choice in what works for you. Qi Dao – Tibetan Shamanic Qigong – should be experienced by all and Lama Tantrapa should be applauded for extending to us means by which we can become more spiritually awakened.

- Karl Ardo, Advanced Instructor/Clinical Qigong Therapist
Producer of *QiGong: A Guide to Well Being*

The practice of Qi Dao is not just another exercise program. It is a process of becoming free and natural. I knew from the first time I met Rinpoche that what he had to offer was very different from anything I had ever experienced before. To my surprise, practicing Qi Dao has far exceeded my expectations. I now live my life with more joy, freedom, and excitement than I ever dreamed possible. If you take the time for yourself, as I did, and continue your exploration of Qi Dao, I'm certain it will transform your life and empower you to manifest your dreams.

- Kali Samaya Tara, JD, Mediator, Certified Qi Dao Coach

Dedication

This book is dedicated to my parents and grandparents, as well as all the past, present and future generations of Qi Dao practitioners.

Acknowledgements

I pay homage to all the spiritual teachers – Tibetan Lamas, Siberian Shamans, Buddhist monks and Qigong Masters – who shared their teachings with me. I express my appreciation of the leaders and members of the USA National Qigong (Chi Kung) Association, who promote and practice Qigong, a wisdom tradition unifying spiritual adventures, healing and martial arts. I acknowledge all my Subud brothers and sisters for creating one of the few spiritual communities free of dogmas, doctrines, tithes, and hierarchy.

My special thanks to Kali Samaya Tara, whose loving support was crucial in manifesting this book, its companion DVD and the Qi Dao Home Study Course.

Read This First

Qi Dao is a system of self-realization that teaches you to rely on your inherent ability to heal, empower and enlighten yourself. It does not involve the diagnosis and treatment of any diseases; therefore, the contents of this book are not intended to be a substitute for professional medical advice. Reading this book should not be used as a substitute for services provided by medical professionals, nor should it prevent you from receiving medical treatment as needed. Before undertaking the study of any wellness discipline, consult with your allopathic or naturopathic physician. You should be aware that when you engage in this practice, you are doing so entirely at your own risk.

"Qi Dao," Tibetan Shamanic Qigong," "The Art of Being in the Flow" and "Harmonious Culture of Movement" are the trademarks of Lama Somananda Tantrapa, which may not be used without his expressed written permission.

Preface

Most people experience "being in the flow" or "in the zone" at least once in their lives. If you have ever had such an amazing experience, you will probably never forget how empowered you felt. Being in the flow allows you to feel the flow of *Qi* – the energy of life. You can learn to perceive the flow of *Qi* in your body and around it; however, trying to manipulate or direct this flow would only waste your time and energy, just like pushing a river upstream. Instead, through the practice of Qi Dao, you can learn to immerse yourself into the flow of life and enjoy it fully.

Using this book and its companion DVD, as well as the entire Qi Dao Home Study Course, you will learn to love yourself and to pay greater attention to your body, movements and energy. As you develop a greater appreciation of your body, you will learn things about yourself you did not know before. Developing your *kinesthetic* awareness – awareness of movement – will hone your sixth sense called *kinesthesia*. Without this awareness of movement you cannot experience life fully, simply because all life is movement.

Awareness of energy will require shifting your attention from the outer forms to the inner essence of everything, starting with yourself. Sensing the resonance of your energy with different opportunities that life presents to you will enable you to choose what works best for you. With practice, you will learn to exercise your freedom, literally, with every step you take on Earth.

You may notice that Qi Dao does not teach you any forms, which allows you to be truly authentic by making choices that resonate with you moment after moment. It will empower you to become more natural and spontaneous as well as to experience a greater sense of well-being and spiritual awakening.

Table of Contents

Introduction

Welcome to my world of Qi Dao, the ancient energy art of Tibetan Shamanic Qigong. My spiritual tradition, named Qi Dao (or *Ch'i Tao* if you like this spelling), which literally means "the path of energy," or "the flow of life force," is a style of Qigong (also spelled *Ch'i Kung*) rooted in the Tibetan Shamanic tradition of self-realization called Bön. Following many generations of Tibetan lamas and Shamans since time immemorial, I explore this magical world where the stuff of myths and legends is quite real. Along my spiritual journey, the miracles of natural healing and amazing feats of power have been common place. I came to believe that everyone practicing this "Adventure Yoga" can receive revelations directly from spirit and learn to follow the inner guidance to enjoy being in the flow of the dream called life.

Have you ever thought that your life journey was meant to be a grand adventure, rather than a misadventure? Perhaps, you are one of those lucky individuals who have experienced "being in the flow" or, as some athletes call it, "in the zone." If you have experienced it, you will probably never forget the profound sense of harmony associated with being in the flow. And if you have never experienced it, at least, you may be able to imagine yourself being empowered, centered and present. Your imagination may be as potent as your memory in preparing you for this exciting adventure in self-realization and learning to live a dream life.

Imagine a world where men and women can travel through life in harmony with each other and the world around them; where every human being can be in touch with his or her inner nature. Everyone there feels confident and free of any artificial limitations that religions, society, or family upbringing tend to impose on people. In such a dream world, everyone has an opportunity to live a healthy and fulfilling lifestyle, enjoying all the abundance life has to offer. Picture yourself in a world where every child and adult can feel empowered to openly experience and explore their greatest potentials, allowing them to blossom fully. In this dream world, the powers that used to be considered paranormal or supernatural are daily occurrences. Now you have a chance to turn your life into a heroic quest to discover the true nature of Being.

Of course, being in the flow is not an exclusive prerogative of Tibetan lamas and top-notch athletes. Virtually every indigenous nation on the face of the Earth has stories about the heroes, whose lives were dedicated to the exploration of the unknown, be that unknown lands or their inner realms. Those spiritual adventurers, regardless of their origins and personal histories, experienced profound transformations and astonishing feats of power that most people could only dream about. In our Qi Dao tribe, we call this way of being "dream being," which means, among other things, experiencing life as though being in a dream. Dream Being is not only a verb, but also a noun representing the source of all your dreams: daydreams as well as night dreams. It is the mystical source of the big dream called life that in many Oriental schools of thought is referred to as the Dao (or *Tao,* if you will).

What is this mystical Dao? It is unseen, but it is everywhere. You may want to know it, but it cannot be intellectually understood. You may strive to find it, even though it has always been within you. "To become one with the Dao" has been the ultimate purpose of meditation retreats, pilgrimages and other spiritual adventures for millennia. Anyone who experiences oneness with the Dao can effortlessly navigate through life, being continuously in the flow, free of attachments, conflicts, or suffering. Nobody can harm or kill such a person, because anyone who would dare to go against him or her would also go against the power of the entire universe. Such an awakened being can fully enjoy the great power and freedom coming from realizing that the daily life and Dream Being are inseparable.

This awareness, however, has hardly anything to do with intellectual cognition or understanding. The more you try to comprehend this by logically thinking about it, the more you employ your linear mind, which will keep you stuck in the head. Trying not to think about it usually does not help either, because, if you try to stop thinking, you must, at least, have thoughts about not thinking. The practice of Qi Dao offers an alternative way to experience a practice of self-realization tailored for spiritual adventurers that is both extremely effective and easy to implement.

You may be asking yourself, "What does it have to do with me? How can reading this book change the way I live my life?" If you live in a modern society, you are likely to be exposed to so much stress and artificial stimulation that you may feel disconnected from your body, a condition often referred to as "being stuck in the head." This can restrict the free flow of *Qi* and limit your availability to life.

Being out of synch with the flow of things in your life may even manifest as depression, disease, or chronic pain. The more disconnected you are, the more discomfort you may experience. This book will teach you to switch from going through one misadventure after another (that are usually perceived as problems causing suffering) to living a dream life filled with genuine adventures that you start perceiving as excellent learning opportunities.

To explore this path, begin by taking small steps, which is always easier than taking large leaps. It is like learning a foreign language. First, you learn the alphabet; then, using the letters as building blocks, you learn to form words. Subsequently, you learn grammar that should enable you to put words together to create sentences. With practice, you will develop an ability to communicate more eloquently with others, who speak this language. The language you will learn with the help of this book is the language of Harmonious Culture of Movement.

I recommend using this book (and the Home Study Course based on this book) in two ways: as a guide for learning to be in the flow, no matter where your journeys may take you, and as a tutorial for mutual coaching with your practice partner or partners, practicing with whom can make your exploration more interactive and fun. In case you purchased this book by itself, I highly recommend watching its companion DVD that is available online at www.qidao.org/dvd101. Upon perusing our website, you may choose to deepen your studies by receiving Qi Dao Coaching from me or one of my apprentices. Moreover, you may choose to join one of the programs offered through Academy of Qi Dao to become a Certified Qi Dao Coach yourself, so you can assist others in transforming their lives into profound spiritual adventures. For more information about the Qi Dao Practitioner Certification Program and to register, please go to www.qidao.org/program101.

Now, you may be wondering, "Do I have to have a partner to practice Qi Dao with?" Of course, you can and are encouraged to practice it on your own whenever you have a chance. It is more fun and challenging, though, to put to rigorous test all the practices you learn, which is much easier to do with another person. That does not have to be the same person all the time, although some continuity usually helps. Besides, when a person gets to experience just a few applications of even the most basic principles of Qi Dao, he or she will likely become curious to find out more. This is where you will be able to launch your coaching career by encouraging that brave soul to become your regular adventure partner.

Can anyone practice Qi Dao together with you? Ideally, I recommend finding a partner who shares your enthusiasm about venturing outside the box, as it were. In other words, your prospect partner must be eager to explore things that are on the edge of his or her comfort zone. On the other hand, this practice can be beneficial to anyone looking for ways to improve the quality of life in general, or one's mobility, flexibility, wellness, and attitude, in particular.

Hundreds of people from all walks of life completed Qi Dao Coaching programs at my Portland Qigong Clinic, which assisted them with self-healing and advice as to finding more harmonious ways of dealing with the challenges on their life journeys. A much greater efficacy of the semi-private sessions attended by two students or a client and an apprentice gave me the reason to recommend that you also practice Qi Dao with a partner. People often commented about feeling the atmosphere of mutual empowerment and encouragement, which is often lacking in a traditional clinical setting. The effectiveness of the Qi Dao approach to dealing with health, relationship, financial, environmental, and other issues, has been proven time and time again.

On a personal note, as the holder of the Qi Dao lineage, I wish to congratulate you for taking the first steps on this path of self-realization. The basics of Qi Dao presented in this book and its companion DVD will provide you with the knowledge of Harmonious Culture of Movement unique to Qi Dao Masters. Once you have mastered these skills through regular practice, you will be able to apply them in every aspect of your life. As pieces of a puzzle, they will come together to give you a vision of the greater picture of the flow of energy in your world. I have no doubt that, once you have experienced the changes that Qi Dao can bring into your life, you will want to explore more advanced applications of this art covered in my forthcoming books, as well as to join our international tribe of fellow spiritual adventurers. I welcome you to enjoy every step on your journey along this path of living your dreams.

Chapter One: Qi Dao Fundamentals

Shamanism is the most ancient spiritual tradition known to humankind. Throughout its history, the human race has evolved significantly in both technology and science, but human nature has never changed. We all have the same primordial spiritual core that we often call our inner essence or spirit. This inner nature is not always apparent, for the wonders of technological and scientific progress tend to distract us more and more from paying attention to our inner nature as well as to the world of nature around us.

Historically, the establishment of organized religions diverted the masses from the ancient Shamanic teachings and practices. Many religious institutions have a tendency to perceive Shamanism as some sort of witchcraft deserving nothing but persecution and extermination. No wonder, nowadays, there is so little remaining from the former worldwide prominence of the Shamanic culture. The resulting inadequacy of human connection with nature has been rather detrimental both to humanity itself and to all forms of life on our planet. Besides the devastation of natural ecosystems and the extinction of many species, we, humans, tend to pay less and less attention to the world within ourselves, which separates us even further from who we really are.

Who are we, really? Are we some foreign intruders trying to colonize and enslave this planet? Are we a product of the games of uncanny forces that turn us into catalysts for our own self-destruction? To answer these and more serious questions, you would need to focus more of your attention inwards. It is exactly what the Shamans used to practice when communing with the spirit world. It is also what all prophets and mystics did when they received any profound visions and revelations. This way of receiving answers to the most challenging questions has been a direct path for many spiritual masters to self-realization and awakening to the truth of our Being. This experience of self-realization is often so transcendental that many mystics who experienced it never became prophets, since they could not even start translating their incredible revelations into the language of the everyday life. Some of them did speak out and shared the remarkable sense of awakening and enlightenment as to the real source of our existence. They became well-known prophets and founding fathers of different spiritual teachings and world religions.

The Shamans of antiquity developed their acute energy awareness for personal development, healing and protection of their tribes. Through years of trial and error, some of them fine-tuned their abilities to shift attention from the outer appearances of things to their energetic nature that is called *Qi* in Chinese, *Prana* in Sanskrit, or *Mana* in Hawaiian. Energy is the essence of all Being, flowing through all things and manifesting in the multitude of forms. The forms of things are basically vessels for their energetic essence. This applies not only to tangible objects, but also to events, relationships, thoughts, etc. Thanks to the diligent transmission of this knowledge through many generations of dedicated practitioners, now we have a method for awakening our dormant ability to perceive the flow of things in our lives and to be in harmony with that flow.

Although origination of Bön – Tibetan Shamanism – is traditionally attributed to legendary Tonpa Shenrab Miwoche, I believe that Shamanism in general was not founded by a particular person but rather naturally evolved and developed throughout many millennia. Every Shaman had to master his or her unique and authentic ways of realizing his/her true nature. Rather than trying to copy someone else's steps, real masters created their own novel ways of self-realization that were geared to their own physique, energy and mentality. In other words, to be a real Shaman is synonymous to being in the flow.

Qigong, an ancient energy art integrating *Qi* – energy awareness – and *Gong* – the practice of mastering it, is a system of self-realization that has been practiced for more than 5,000 years. Its numerous styles and schools developed mostly along the lines of different philosophical and spiritual traditions in the pursuit of embodiment of their respective teachings. The deeper you explore the history of Qigong in search of its roots, the more apparent it becomes that all of these teachings emerged originally from the vast pool of pre-historic Shamanic practices. Most Qigong styles were organized by and for the followers of one belief system or another in ancient China, Tibet, Mongolia and Korea. Following the establishment of the main Eastern schools of thought about 2,500 years ago, Qigong eventually developed six distinctive branches: Daoist, Buddhist, Tantric, Therapeutic, Wushu (martial arts), and Kung Fu Tze (Confucian) Qigong.

Each of them developed their teachings and methods of training following the steps of their respective founders. The history of some traditions can be traced back to particular individuals who originated their schools of thought, oftentimes even unbeknownst to themselves. As Jesus Christ was not a Christian and Buddha Shakyamuni was not a Buddhist, so most original masters of Yoga and Qigong had no idea that their disciples would institutionalize their personal practices of self-realization. The masters simply followed their own inner guidance as to how to be in the flow of things in this magical world. With time, a lot of people perceived those masters as great examples of living in the flow. The consequent generations of students, however, grew further and further apart from the roots of their respective traditions by institutionalizing them.

About 2,500 years ago, the prominent Chinese philosopher Lao Tze presumably wrote Dao De Jing, which brought together many pieces of the ancient Oriental wisdom and formed the foundation of Daoism. The adherents of that teaching created Daoist Qigong dedicated to the attainment of great longevity and, supposedly, immortality. Around the same period of time, the followers of the famous Chinese philosopher Kung Fu Tze (a.k.a. Confucius) formulated Confucian Qigong, mainly concerned with mentoring leaders and guiding them in creating a harmonious society. Around the same time in India, Buddha Shakyamuni taught his teachings to thousands of devoted disciples, who eventually started practicing Buddhist Qigong to achieve spiritual awakening, or *Nirvana*. The adepts of Tantra, a mystical sect of Hinduism that spread via the Himalayas into Tibet, came up with Tantric Qigong dedicated to self-realization through the means of enlightening personal and transpersonal relationships. Therapeutic Qigong, initially a cornerstone of Oriental Medicine, is mostly concerned with the issues of health and holistic healing. Martial, or Wushu Qigong, as the name implies, is focused on effective self-defense and protection of others.

Nowadays, many Qigong styles are still confined within the parameters of their respective doctrines, while others integrate some aspects of two or more branches of Qigong. For example, Buddhist monks from the Shaolin Temple are known for both martial arts prowess and competence in Buddhist Qigong. Many Daoist Qigong masters are also great healers and/or martial artists. In fact, Tai Chi Chuan is an offspring of Daoist martial arts. By the same token, Tantra is a major part of Buddhist tradition in Tibet and Mongolia where lamas (Shamans and Buddhist spiritual teachers) often integrate Tantric and Buddhist Qigong practices.

There is one style, however, that does not merely try to reach for the fruits on the ends of the branches of the "Qigong tree," but rather goes back to the Shamanic roots of the entire tree and empowers its practitioners to stay true to the original universality of the art. Its practice allows advancing to high levels of achievement in all six applications of Qigong as a result of integrating the power and wisdom of the six branches into one. This non-sectarian tradition of Tibetan Shamanic Qigong has been preserved through the centuries by twenty-seven generations of masters who explored numerous possible applications of energy awareness in all spheres of life, from fighting to healing and sexual energy arts.

Our system has been known under several different names, depending on the culture and language of the person you speak to. In Tibetan, it may be referred to as *Trul Khor*, but in the States, I prefer to use the Chinese name Qi Dao, due to the issues with the Tibetan pronunciation (which really sounds like "true whore"). It originated from an ancient Shamanic tradition called Bön that existed for many millennia prior to the introduction of Buddhism in Tibet by Padmasambhava.

Historically, Tibetan culture did not exist in as much isolation as many Westerners seem to think. Both Indian and Chinese influences have been very strong in Tibet for centuries; without them there would be no Tibetan Buddhism as such. Over the centuries, Qi Dao developed into a refined distillation of the ancient Bön traditions, Indian yogic practices and Chinese energy arts. It has many similarities with a number of other systems such as Tummo, Yantra Yoga and Tai Chi Chuan.

The Mongols, who are culturally close to the Tibetans, disseminated Bön throughout Asia when Genghis Khan and his descendants created the largest empire in human history. As all empires eventually collapse, the Mongol Empire also fell apart 300 years later, and different parts of it became primarily Christian

(Russia), Muslim (Central Asia), Hindu (India), Buddhist (Tibet and Mongolia), or Daoist/Buddhist/Confucian (China). Siberia ended up as the only part of the vast empire where the Siberian Shamanism smoothly blended with the Tibetan/Mongolian traditions and survived to the present day.

During the existence of the Soviet Union, it was quite difficult to perpetuate our practice, since the Communist regime persecuted all types of spirituality and even outlawed all martial arts, fearing that the common people might experience any kind of empowerment. Being born and raised in the former Soviet Union, I experienced on my own skin the brunt of the Communist oppression. Many years ago, the Soviet KGB even gave my Grandfather, from whom I learned most of my skills, an ultimatum: "You must work for us or else..." Well, they used to send people to Siberia, but if you were already living there, what else do you think they might do to punish you for non-cooperation? Reluctantly, he agreed to train the top echelon of the KGB, including Stalin's bodyguards.

Many aspects of our tradition can be seen in the Systema – the Russian martial arts developed by such masters as Mikhail Ryabko and Alexei Kadochnikov, both of whom trained the Russian Special Forces, too. If you have an opportunity to experience that art in action, you will find it very fluid and formless, quite distinct from the vast majority of the Chinese, Japanese and Korean styles of martial arts, but very similar to Qi Dao. As you can imagine, it would have been totally suicidal to teach any spiritual aspects of our art to the Soviet spooks; that is why the most profound parts of Qi Dao cannot be found in the Systema.

Bruce Kumar Frantzis, a well-known American Qigong master, pointed out to me a few years ago that I might want to call my teachings Shen Gong (spiritual practice) rather than Qigong (energy practice), because it is ultimately dedicated to self-realization and awakening to the dream-like nature of reality instead of focusing on the cultivation and manipulation of *Qi* as in most styles of Chinese Qigong. My respect to Mr. Frantzis notwithstanding, I continue referring to Qi Dao as Tibetan Shamanic Qigong, whose foundational principles are the subject of this chapter.

Being Natural

Being natural requires paying attention to the inner nature of all things rather than their forms. When most people think of Qigong, they usually think of "doing forms" – sets of choreographed movements practiced repetitively. I do not believe that the sages of antiquity, who originated Qigong thousands of years ago, had to study any "forms." Those masters created their systems of self-realization not by practicing some forms, but by discovering their own, authentic ways to experience their true nature. Since they were the original founders, they had no human teachers to emulate. They had to learn from Mother Nature as well as their inner nature. The founders of the oldest systems of self-realization had to rely on the knowledge gathered from their own personal experiences and some anecdotal stories about the miraculous powers of the ancient Shamans. They had to find empirically their own unique methods of being in the flow of *Qi* and experimenting with it. Such a genuine approach reared great Qigong masters, whose mastery was based on personal observation and exploration, rather than a routine repetition of forms. Playing with each other and with different animals was the testing ground for their skills and powers.

Alas, the tendency of the human mind to be focused on appearances instead of the inner essence eventually reduced many styles of Qigong, as well as Yoga, Kung Fu, Tai Chi, etc., to merely "doing forms." You would be hard pressed to find anyone who managed to achieve anything profound by emulating their teachers' external appearances. In order to experience the authentic mastery of being in the flow, you will need to start by shifting attention from forms to the true essence of everything, starting with your own inner nature, which is pure energy.

Comparing yourself to others is such an insidious tendency that many artists never transcend the stage of mimicking their role models. Yet the entire idea of mastery implies being natural in your art and authentic in your artistic expression. Qi Dao teaches you to develop an attitude of authenticity from the very beginning while allowing yourself to be natural.

Since change is the most constant thing in the universe, **the flow is always different from one person to another and from one moment to another**. This means that to copy the master's movements or other actions is to grasp the form of the master's experience rather than the essence. Such imitation would not enable anyone to be in the flow, because being in the flow implies being in one's own flow, not in someone else's flow. Through the practice of Qi Dao you will learn to be truly authentic by perceiving the flow of life force within you and throughout the world around you. You will learn to surrender to the flow and allow it to guide you in whatever way is appropriate. It will allow you to manifest your dreams effortlessly and gracefully.

This is precisely what the Founder of Aikido, O-Sensei Morihei Ueshiba, did when he created (perhaps, unbeknownst to himself) a superb style of Internal Martial Arts geared toward dealing with attacks by opponents stuck in their heads. Virtually all Aikido techniques operate from the energy center in the pelvis often referred to as Lower *Dan Tien,* or *Hara* in Japanese, which conducts the energy of the element of Water. In Aikido, *Atemi* (distracting counter-attack) is most often directed towards the head because it is where the attackers get their energy as long as they operate on the energy of the element of Earth. In fact, exhibiting aggression is an indication of being stuck in the Upper *Dan Tien* or another energy center. It often takes just a slight slap in the face to recycle this energy or even to turn the energy center off. Then it becomes so much easier to throw the opponent on the ground utilizing his or her own inertia and lack of balance.

An interesting example of being natural when challenged by someone familiar with the element of Water can be found in Yi Chuan, a modern style of Internal Martial Arts founded by Wang Xiangzhai. Similar to Tai Chi Chuan, the practice of Yi Chuan incorporates *Tui Shou* (often translated as "pushing hands"), a method of transcending opposition and establishing perception of your opponent as your adventure partner. In fact, the practice of *Tui Shou* is mostly about energy awareness, rather than physical pushing. It is about developing acute sensitivity and ability to move with the flow of the opponent's *Qi* (paradoxically, Wang Xiangzhai did not teach his students that *Qi* was used in Yi Chuan). Seemingly slow movements do carry a lot of power, though this power is not to be used against the opponent's attack, but along his vector of force just slightly redirecting him to miss his aim. Following this principle, the one who pushes harder, as a rule, has less balance and must quickly choose whether to relax standing or on the ground.

Being Attentive

One of the multiple translations of Dao De Jing states:

"To experience without intention is to sense the world;

To experience with intention is to anticipate the world."

Replacing intention with attention is a crucial prerequisite for being in the flow. When you are driven by your desires, you negate the present by striving to achieve what you think will be better than what is present. Every intention is based on expectations, projections and/or judgments. Since life never seems to meet expectations, intentions set you up for disappointment and suffering. Letting go of intentions and becoming attentive allows you to be more present.

Attention is the interface between what you know and what you do not know. You cannot learn without paying attention, since you cannot remember that which you pay no attention to. Development of attention always requires acceptance. Being attentive is only possible when you accept what is. You cannot be attentive to something you do not accept, simply because when you are not accepting it, you are busy resisting it or running away from it, engaging in "fight or flight" instead of just being present. Such lack of acceptance creates the rigid dualism of right and wrong, judgment of actions and threats of adverse consequences. For instance, when you label something as "good," you may create an expectation that it should be good not only for you but also for others. It may also imply an expectation of continuous goodness or badness despite any common sense. Many things that were deemed good yesterday may not be so good today and what resonates with one person may not resonate for others. Labeling something "bad" is just as misleading. Being accepting will help you transcend this dualism, allowing you to be more content and happy with your life.

Your practice of Qi Dao must begin by learning to shift from the mode of having attention to the mode of being attentive. This entails learning how to be fully accepting of what is; being present and awake to the reality that is unfolding right in front of you and within you moment by moment. It requires letting go of expectations, projections, and judgments of things or persons as good or bad. As you practice, you will learn to pay attention to the flow of *Qi* and to be in the flow.

Through the practice of Qi Dao you will learn to enjoy less doing and more being. This means that you do not always need to do something to manifest your dreams. For example, **people usually heal when they are ready to heal**. The process of re-discovering health and wellness depends more on being open and available to life, than on doing any deliberate healing practices. Awareness is particularly crucial in this process, since your health, relationships, spiritual and other issues can only get efficiently resolved when you are receptive to the lessons presented by those issues. Your readiness to embody vibrant health and wellbeing promotes a greater sense of being in the flow and empowers you to "awaken the healer within," as my friend Dr. Roger Jahnke puts it. This requires that you develop an intimate awareness of the *somatic* (bodily) manifestations of your identity and beliefs.

"Yi Dao Qi Dao" is a common Chinese expression among Qigong practitioners that means: **"where awareness (or attention) goes, energy flows."** It mostly applies to beginners though, while advanced practitioners and Qigong masters learn to follow the reversal principle – *Qi Dao Yi Dao* – **"Wherever energy flows, awareness follows."** In other words, mastery of being in the flow entails transition from moving or projecting energy to going with the flow of *Qi* and being in the flow.

Many people in the modern society live in the mode of striving to have attention and thriving on the energy of attention they receive from others. You probably know people willing to do, say or wear whatever it takes to receive as much attention as possible. It certainly feels good to have attention. Since attention can direct energy, you get energized when you receive attention. Why is this pattern of behavior so pervasive? Some blame Western society, which provides no role models of attentiveness. Actually, this pattern keeps repeating itself because people have a habit of forgetting that they have an abundant source of attention within them. If you think about it, you will realize that **nobody can give you as much attention as you can give yourself.** When you do so, you recycle a constant flow of energy within your energy system, which gives you an access to an abundance of *Qi* within you.

Being in the Flow

Imagine coming to a crossroads and feeling the energies of different directions you could choose. You may notice that your energy resonates with some directions better than others. Where there is resonance, your energy is attracted to flow in that direction. If you pay attention to such resonance, you can allow the flow of life to unfold naturally and spontaneously. But if you do not pay attention to this resonance, you may feel compelled to take a path based on your preconceived ideas or stereotypes. Rather than following your own ideas, you may be indoctrinated to conform to traditional beliefs or stereotypes handed down from past generations. Letting go of such programming is not simply an intellectual exercise but rather a process of discovering mental alertness, spiritual openness and authenticity. These qualities can empower you to reconnect with the flow of life and promote freedom of choice.

When you imagine yourself at a crossroad, you are in a position where you have the freedom to choose your direction. Personal freedom is necessary to be able to make a choice in any situation of this sort. Your freedom, however, may often be restricted by some beliefs distorting your perception. If you follow the beliefs that do not promote your perception of the flow, they become an impediment to being in the flow. Therefore, you may need to look into your belief system to check which beliefs resonate with your consciousness and which ones do not.

One of the central beliefs that promotes being in the flow is the belief that **everything always happens exactly the way it has to happen.** Perhaps you had some experiences in your life that were dramatic or even traumatic at the time. With time, maybe even years later, you might realize that you actually became wiser due to having had those difficult experiences under your belt. As it were, what did not kill you really did make you stronger. Moreover, the energy of the circumstances of your life and its flow at that particular time had to match the energy of the event; otherwise, there would have been no way for the event to manifest. If you wish that things went differently for you in the past, consider that they actually would have been different only if your energy had been different. Indeed, your awareness and beliefs have everything to do with your energy moment by moment.

You can apply the same awareness to the present time as well as the future. Everything is and will be manifesting according to the resonance of energies involved. You may even observe the process of manifestation by paying attention to your energy, including your psychological state, beliefs and quality of attention, which you are ultimately free to choose. As you will discover through observation, nobody is doing anything to anyone, we manifest our own realities according to our current energy. Once you have learned to stop taking everything personally, thus dissolving your energetic chains, nothing will be able to prevent you from experiencing much greater degrees of freedom. At the same time, you will learn to question reality and give yourself an affirmation that life is a dream. This will enable you to relate to everything you perceive as energy and learn to feel the flow of the energy everything is made of in the dream called life.

Struggling against the flow of a night dream is a sure way to turn it into a nightmare. Similarly, if you struggle against the flow of your daily life, you single-handedly turn your life into a nightmare. Going against the flow of things only exhausts your energy, takes a toll on your health, and wastes your time. As soon as you realize that **life's challenges can be perceived as learning opportunities rather than problems**, you will become less tense or "stressed-out" and find yourself in the flow of life. Being in the flow will empower you to live a dream life for real.

Being Awake

Being awake is somewhat similar to the sense of awakening to the reality of dreaming when you become lucid in a night dream. Lucidity – being awake to the reality of your dreams during the process of dreaming – can teach you a great deal about life in general. Just think about it: most of your knowledge about life has to be based on your memories and everything you know about your dreams is based on memories, too. Since you use the same memory mechanism in knowing about both your dreams and your daily life, the distinction between dreaming and waking is essentially illusory. Indeed, being fully awake in daily life is very much like being lucid in a night dream.

Consider what everything in the world of dreaming is made of. However tangible, heavy, or solid things may appear in your dreams, all of them are made of nothing other than pure energy. What else could they possibly be made of? Similarly, as modern physicists echo the sages of all ages, everything in the world of "waking life" is essentially made of energy, too. Analogies between dreaming and daily worlds can continue *ad infinitum*.

Imagine an iceberg – a tiny part of it is visible above the surface of the water while its massive main part is hidden deep under water. In a similar fashion, everything you know about yourself, whatever you may refer to as your self, including your personal history, character, ideas and beliefs, is just a little tip of the iceberg. Whatever you do not know about yourself, as well as all your unmanifest potentials and dreams, constitutes the underwater part of the iceberg that supports and manifests the existence of the tip. The deeper part of the iceberg is connected underwater with all the other icebergs – everyone and everything in the whole world. They are not separate from you but rather interdependent and interconnected by the means of energy fields that everything is made of. We are all interconnected dream beings – the facets of the universal Dao – like waves that are inseparable from the ocean. You may feel as though you are a separate entity, but to perceive a wave as an independent entity is certainly an illusion.

When having a lucid dream, you can recognize that everything and everyone in the world of dreaming are projections of your own consciousness. Every dream character represents a certain part of your consciousness that you may not be willing to identify with, so you dream it up as an entity separate from you. Being totally awake in the world of dreaming encourages you to accept every single aspect of your dreaming. Even when you dream up anyone or anything challenging you in your dreams, they enact certain disconnected parts of yourself that are trying to get your attention. They may feel disempowered due to a lack of attention they receive; once you start being attentive to them, they will be able to manifest their dreams of healing and empowerment. **The more parts of yourself you help to manifest their dreams, the more they will help you manifest yours.** You may discover that some aspects of yourself have been split off so that you can learn about them and fully reintegrate them into the wholeness of your being.

Since everything in both dreams and in daily life is made of the same universal energy, you can learn to be in the flow of life in the same fashion as you learn to be in the flow of energy in dreaming. With practice, you will learn to recognize that everything and everyone in your daily life are also projections of the dreaming mind. It is your Dream Being dreaming up the entire world as you dream up everything in your dreams. It is that deeper part of you that manifests not only your precious self but also the entire world as you know it. It is both the deeper part of you as well as the deeper part of each and every one of us. **If you think that you live in a stupid world full of stupid people, it is high time to wake up!** You cannot awaken anyone other than yourself, for everyone in your "waking life" is your dream character. Becoming awake will invite you to start relating to people and things around you in a very different way – aware of the inherent oneness of everything in the holographic universe of your being, Dream Being that is.

Most interestingly, awakening is not a one shot kind of a deal, because even after the most profound awakenings, we all have the tendency to fall asleep over and over again. Although this process has its own ebb and flow, you can catch and ride a wave of awakening by consciously identifying with the creator of the dream, the dreamer of the dream drama you call your life. Becoming one with the dreamer will encourage you to accept full responsibility for your destiny as well as empower you to manifest a more creative and abundant life for yourself and all your dream characters.

I would summarize self-realization as realizing that **the source of your individual dreams is the same as the mystical source of the big dream called life.**

Lama Somananda Tantrapa

Chapter Two: The Basics of Harmonious Culture of Movement

When learning Qi Dao, you will find it invaluable to have one or more partners to practice with. Together with your practice partners you are invited to experiment with all the principles of Qi Dao, putting each and every one of them to rigorous test. It will provide you with total confidence, which you would never get out of blindly following any forms or some magical formulas. Confidence built on the foundation of personal experience and observation will empower you to make your own choices and decisions.

Almost anyone can be coached in this art as long as they are willing to be coachable. This also applies to your practice partners – let them make their own choices without imposing your will. You will see how much happier they are when they follow through with their own choices rather than any choices made by you or anyone else.

Even when giving suggestions for establishing your regular practice, I prefer to provide guidelines instead of imposing steadfast rules:

- Find the place and time that is convenient for you and your adventure partner(s) – just working out the logistics of your practice may become an experiment in being in the flow
- Start exploring slowly, adding more challenging practices as you progress

- Get creative with your regimen by adapting the order, number and pace of your explorations to match your state of mind, energy and physique
- Coach yourself, since you are the world authority on your life – let the practice itself become your teacher
- Do not push beyond your comfort zone until you are ready to transcend it
- Keep your practice simple and fun.

Now, let us explore how you can apply the body-mind awareness to promote a natural and effortless state of being. This state facilitates balance, which is only possible with the alignment of all parts of the body and mind. You are about to learn to maintain the integrity of your organism at all times and to facilitate wellness and a healthy lifestyle by finding harmony with the flow of energy within and around you.

Natural Stance

Natural Stance, as the name implies, is the simplest way to stand naturally. A naturally balanced human body responds to the challenge of gravity by bringing itself to a stable position using its bone structure to support its weight and prevent falling. Streamlining of the torso allows the body to spend the least amount of energy to maintain a stable, upright stance.

If you are one of the many people leading a sedentary lifestyle you may not know how to keep your body naturally balanced and aligned. If you deviate from your natural alignments, the weight of your body will not be supported by its bone structure, and you will have to engage your muscles to keep yourself from falling. Although muscular tension may prevent you from falling, **muscles are never as strong as bones; muscles spend energy while the bones do their work effortlessly**. Not only will this make you tired but it will also restrict your mobility and cause discomfort. Eventually, chronically tense muscles will begin to ache from the effort required to keep the misaligned body from falling.

If the body is misaligned, it may try various compensation strategies (e.g., shift the weight between the hips, tilt the pelvis, bend the spine, raise one shoulder or the other, etc.), all of which will eventually contribute to muscular tension and pain. Learning Natural Stance and addressing the issue of balance between the feet can often help resolve such common conditions as headache, backache, shoulder pain, *sciatica*, and even *scoliosis*.

In Natural Stance, the weight of the body is distributed evenly between both legs while the torso and head are resting on the bone structure of the spine. The natural curve of the spine is neither exaggerated nor diminished. This allows the free flow of energy throughout the organism. If you could visualize the energy field of such a Streamlined person, their energy field would appear Symmetrical and Centered.

You can experience Natural Stance by jumping up in the air and landing on both feet as softly as possible with your feet about shoulder-width apart. Notice that the easiest way to do this is to land with you knees bent, letting your *quadriceps* (thigh muscles) absorb the shock of landing. They are, after all, the largest muscles in the human body that are most suitable for being shock absorbers. Natural Stance allows you to maintain natural body alignment, distributing most of your weight on the bone structure of your body, rather than the muscles.

Taking a Natural Stance

Notice how bent your knees are. Naturally, the deeper you squat, the further the toes tend to turn outwards away from the Centerline with the knees following suit. Experiment with bending your knees enough to cover your feet when you look at them. Ask your practice partner to test how stable you are in this stance. Compare this to other positions, where your knees would not cover your feet from sight.

Taking a Natural Stance is an exercise in awareness in its own right. It is an excellent way to begin each of the explorations presented in this book. Please remember to keep checking your alignments throughout your practice and whenever you can in your daily life.

Body Awareness

In the English language, there are many metaphors reflecting the awareness of the human body-mind. For example, some people can be "straight," "bent," "crooked," "high- or lowbrow." Others may appear "nosey," "spineless," "gutless," or, say, "heartless." Sometimes people "face things," "throw their weight around," "turn their back" on a problem, "wash hands," or even "lose face." You may say that one has "a good head on one's shoulders," "a stiff upper lip," or "no leg to stand on." Moreover, a person may appear to have "balls of steel," "butterflies in the stomach," "a chip on one's shoulder," or even "a stick up one's ass."

These phrases hint at some degree of body awareness people had in the olden days. You have to pay at least some attention to your bodily sensations and expressions in order to come up with such body-centered phraseology. Nowadays, people seem to pay less attention to their bodies than their cars or computers. It appears that the advancements in technology have left our "civilized world" without the need to pay attention to the sacred abode of our precious lives. Being in the flow of life within the temple you inhabit – the physical body and its energy field – is the hallmark premise of Qi Dao.

Alignment of the Head

Aligning the head

Alignments of the head and neck are obvious areas to start with. People in modern society often complain about pain and tension in the neck and the base of the skull. Such tension blocks the circulation of blood and lymph and often leads to headaches, ringing in the ears, *temporo-mandibular* joint *(TMJ)* dysfunction, eyesight disorders and other complaints. Observation suggests that energy cannot flow freely through areas of the body holding a lot of tension. Since communication requires free flow of energy, tension in the neck and shoulders restricts and even disconnects communication between the head and the rest of the body.

The phrase "stuck in the head" generally denotes someone who thinks or intellectualizes too much. At the same time, it describes a person whose muscular tension has created an energetic and emotional divide between the head and the rest of the body. Someone who is stuck in the head often displays a peculiar culture of movement revealing his or her body awareness, or rather lack thereof. I usually refer to such a culture of movement as disharmonious, because it isolates and compartmentalizes movements of different parts of the body, which makes it look really robotic.

For the energy to flow freely between the head and the rest of the body, the neck and shoulders need to be free of excessive tension. When the head and neck are misaligned, the muscles of the neck have to continuously hold tension in order to compensate for the lack of support from the spine. When the *vertebrae* of the neck naturally rest one on top of the other, there is no need for any more tension than a regular muscular tone. **Since the *cervical* spine is a part of the whole spine, you cannot be in alignment if your head and neck are not aligned.** Neck alignment requires some basic awareness of its bone structure. Despite popular belief, the *cervical vertebrae* are not really close to the back of the neck, like many people think, confusing the *vertebrae* for their *spinous processes*, but are connected to the center of the *skull* and continue down in the middle of the neck.

Head alignment also entails awareness of the top of the head so that it actually is the highest point of the head. The center of mass of the head corresponds to the location of the *atlas* – the first *cervical vertebra*. The head can balance effortlessly on the bone structure of the neck when it is in a neutral position. It happens totally naturally as long as the top of your head (*Bai Hui* acupressure point) is literally on top.

In order to experience the natural alignment of your head, you can gently pull your head straight up by the tips of the ears with your fingers. Notice the way your head naturally finds its alignment. Bear in mind that tension is something you do to yourself. Keeping the head out of its natural alignment requires a lot of doing. You cannot ease tension by doing more. **Relaxation is a function of non-doing.** By simply paying attention to the areas of tension in your body, you will begin to notice changes happening moment by moment.

Experiment with the following methods of focusing attention on any tense muscles:

1) Physical touch – match tension with pressure and gradually ease pressure when the tension begins to subside;
2) Increasing and decreasing tension – prevent the head from moving with the help of one or both hands while contracting the tense muscles even more and then relaxing them;
3) Animation of the head – move your head with the help of the hands in the direction it wants to go (wherever the tense muscles try to pull it) without using the neck muscles at all;
4) Breathing and visualization – imagine that you can breathe through your neck muscles while observing the flow of energy being restored.

No need to force *Qi* to flow where you think it should flow or to do anything to the muscles in attempt to make them relax, unless you actually wish to experience more stress and frustration. **Letting go of tension goes hand-in-hand with letting go of expectations.**

Alignment of the Arms

Exploring the alignment of the arms

Before exploring alignment of the arms, ask your partner to pull your arms down by the wrists, as you stand upright. Notice the difference in the amount of tension in your shoulders and upper back when the palms are facing forward versus when they are facing backwards. Since the palm is the front of the hand (the back of the hand is obviously its back), it makes a difference whether it faces forward or backwards. In Qi Dao, we say that **when the backs of your hands are**

facing forward, you are wearing your arms backwards, which may be almost as uncomfortable as wearing your legs backwards.

Most people experience more tension in the shoulders and upper back when they turn their palms backwards. This tension is often habitual and not within your conscious awareness. To test whether it takes tension to wear the arms backwards, ask your partner to apply gentle pressure on your *deltoids* (shoulder muscles) while you turn your palm all the way back and forth.

Pronation (turning the palm backwards) requires contracting the *anterior deltoid* and shifts the shoulder joint forward from its naturally aligned position. As a result, you may slouch, rounding the shoulders and projecting the head forward. With the weight of the head no longer supported by the bone structure of the neck, the muscles in the back of the neck will have to work overtime. The chronic tension of the *trapezius* and other shoulder muscles is often a product of this misalignment.

Supination (turning the palm forward) can be experienced without contracting the shoulder muscles, but rather allowing your shoulders to relax. After experimenting with all the possible options, notice which alignment of the arms feels more natural for you and allow your body to follow your insight.

If you attempt to force your palms to face forward while maintaining your habitual tension, you will have to counter it by tensing up your *teres major* (the muscle connecting the *scapula* and *humerus* bones of the upper arm). This will only give you twice the amount of tension as before. Alignment of your arms requires non-doing – no longer holding tension in your *deltoids*.

Alignment of the Legs

People often complain about pain in the feet, knees, or hips. Such pain is usually a result of the misalignment of their legs. To find out about the natural alignment of your legs, ask your partner to gently push into your kneecap from the direction in which your toes are pointing while you are standing in the Natural Stance. Notice whether it is easier to push you off balance when the knee is pointing in the same direction as the toes or when it is pointing elsewhere.

Generally speaking, **an aligned leg has the toes and knee pointing in the same direction**. If you are standing with your knees locked, however, this alignment will not be so apparent and you will be easy to push over whichever way you turn your toes. To learn about your leg alignment, you can use a simple rule of thumb: glance down and see whether your knees cover your toes from sight when in the Natural Stance.

Exploring the alignment of the legs

If you are one of the curious folks who really want to find out which of the five toes needs to be in alignment with the knee, I invite you to experiment with some subtle shifting side-to-side in order to figure this our for yourself. Since everyone's body is unique and different, I see no reason to establish any uniform rules for body alignments. Besides, exploration is what provides you with opportunities for developing your own authentic body awareness, rather than blindly following someone else's rules.

Alignment of the legs will make an immediate difference in the way the weight is distributed on the feet. The balance of the whole body will change if you shift the weight side-to-side or back and forth on each foot. Your partner can easily test your overall balance by pushing you in the stomach. The results of such tests will depend significantly upon the alignment of your legs. If your knees do not cover your toes from sight, your foot, lower and upper leg will not be in the same plane. This will weaken your balance making you easy to push over.

To improve your balance, experiment with distribution of your weight between the inner and outer edges of each foot as well as between the toes and heels.

When the weight is on the outer edge of the foot, the knee is likely to be *everted* (turned outwards); and when the weight is on the inner edge of the foot, the knee is likely to be *inverted* (turned inwards). With practice, you will learn to maintain a natural alignment of the legs and feel Grounded even without looking at your feet. Just feel the way your feet touch the ground paying attention to your weight distribution while standing or moving. Awareness gained through this exploration will surely enhance your balance and overall wellness.

Alignment of the Torso

Exploring torso alignment

Just like the alignments of your head and limbs, alignment of your torso is crucial for your health and well-being. **A naturally aligned human body has maximum stability and balance and is free of tension.**

As the key alignment, torso alignment affects the alignments of all the other parts of the body and vice-versa. When you stand, your torso needs to be balanced on the support system of the legs. If your body's weight is habitually distributed on one leg more than the other, the pelvis will have a tendency to tilt away from the weight-bearing leg. This tilt of the pelvis will inevitably create a curve in the lower or *lumbar* spine. To compensate for this misalignment, the muscles on the weight-bearing side will have a tendency to pull the upper or *thoracic* spine in the opposite direction bringing the shoulder down on the same side. The neck will usually compensate by pulling away from the lower shoulder. Such habitual shifting of the weight away from the Center may result in developing a chronic pattern of holding tension in your body (see the chapter on Holding Patterns).

Ask your practice partner to test your stability by gently pushing your hips from one side and then, with an equal amount of effort, from the other. Notice whether your stability is more challenged when being pushed from one side versus the other. Then slowly shift your weight side to side in order to feel which side habitually bears more weight. Notice an increase in tension in the side muscles when shifting the weight off Center on that respective side, as well as relaxation when returning to the Centered position. As you experiment with slowly rocking your pelvis, pay particular attention to the position of your center of mass associated with relaxation of both sides, for this is where your torso is most aligned and Centered.

Do not forget to check whether your pelvis habitually tilts forward or backward – this may be an invitation to explore your alignment in the frontal plane of your body. Slowly thrust your pelvis back and forth noticing alternating tensions in the muscles of your lower back and abdomen. Pay specific attention to the point of rest in the middle, when both of those groups of muscles relax. That is the Neutral position of the pelvis that aligns the spine and requires the least amount of tension and effort to support your body upright. The weight of your entire upper body can peacefully rest on your skeletal structure as long as it is in alignment.

I would like you to explore a famous Qigong exercise called *Zhan Zhuang*, or "standing like a tree," which is a type of standing meditation dedicated to finding the sense of physical and mental equanimity. You can experience it standing in a Natural Stance and observing your breath as well as different degrees of tension in various muscles throughout your body. Unlike some Qigong styles that prescribe standing at certain times of the day, facing particular directions, Qi Dao does not impose any rigid rules but rather invites you to experiment and find out for yourself what works better for you. For more detailed explanations combined with a guided meditation, please listen to the Qi Dao Initiation CD that is also included in our

Home Study Course available online at www.qidao.org/course101. After some practice, once you have found a way to enjoy standing still, you will be able to expand this feeling by discovering effortlessness in motion.

Kinesthetic Awareness

Kinesthetic awareness – the sense of movement – is your real sixth sense, in addition to vision, hearing, smell, taste and touch. Sadly, *kinesthesia* is not even a part of most people's vocabulary. If you do not know what to call an experience, how much attention will you pay to it?

The sense of movement is the only way to experience first-hand the relationship between space and time. It gives you the direct experience of life. Many people only experience life through their visual and/or auditory senses. This externalizes their experience, making it second-hand. They just observe life happen instead of participating in it. This is characteristic of the culture of watching TV, voyeurism and a sedentary lifestyle, which is rampant in the civilized countries. Since there cannot be any life without movement, **in order to experience life, one needs to experience movement**.

If we spend many hours a day sitting, we eventually forget about the body and its needs. Without experiencing movement, we develop *kinesthetic amnesia*, forgetting how to relate to our own body. The body also forgets how to support itself and move gracefully and effortlessly. Instead, it develops patterns of movement based on robotic, linear and jerky movements. These patterns are not efficient, from the point of view of body mechanics, as they require greater expenditures of energy. They promote being "stuck in the head" instead of promoting a harmonious flow of energy between the head and the rest of the body.

One of my students, who in the beginning appeared seriously stuck in her head, when asked to lift one foot for a moment without shifting her weight onto the other foot, replied that it would be humanly impossible. Up to that moment, her belief system did not allow her to perform such an "impossible" maneuver. I had to resort to quoting Henry Ford: "Whether you believe you can or you can't, you're right." Only after my demonstration of a Natural Step did she realize that her beliefs were the only limitation preventing her from moving like that!

Natural Steps Side to Side

It is usually easier to progress (literally and figuratively) using small steps rather than large leaps. Qi Dao teaches us to accomplish things with small, practical steps. All of our basic practices involve steps small enough to maintain full awareness and control of our motion. In just about any challenging situation we encounter in the practice of Qi Dao, we can proceed more gracefully with small steps rather than either freezing with fear and tension, like a deer in the headlights of a car, or recklessly leaping ahead. As with most Qi Dao principles, letting go of "fight or flight" reactivity can be applied throughout your daily life.

Taking a Natural Step sideways

Natural Step is a method of moving with small steps in the most efficient and quickest fashion. While in Natural Stance, choose to move either to the right or to the left using the foot corresponding to the chosen direction. Lift that foot off the ground without shifting your weight onto the other foot and allow the force of gravity to propel you sideways. Landing on the entire surface of the sole of the stepping foot requires keeping the knees soft and relaxed. After you softly land that foot on the ground, complete your Natural Step by bringing the other foot closer to the first one to resume a comfortable Natural Stance.

As you move sideways, also notice how you can observe the Symmetry of your body. This principle is particularly wise to observe when your legs are spread out sideways to any degree. Your body is Symmetrical when the angles between the axis of your body and the legs are the same on both sides of your body.

The principle of Symmetry is also relevant whenever the torso tilts sideways away from its vertical alignment. Slide your hands down your thighs to check this alignment when stepping sideways. For example, if your right hand reaches closer to the right knee than the other hand at any moment during the Natural Step to the right, it means that your body is tilting excessively to the right. Obviously, the same can be said for the left side, as long as your arms are about the same length.

When you begin exploring more advanced applications of Qi Dao, you will see that this applies to practicing certain kicks, too. As you raise one leg, your entire torso needs to tilt half as far to the opposite side for balance. This way, you can actually keep your head at more or less the same height rather than bobbing up and down while stepping or kicking.

Practice using this Natural Step sideways in the one direction, then reverse and travel in the opposite direction. I believe that it is essential to be equally capable of moving in either direction with the same degree of gracefulness. This movement requires no physical effort, but simply uses the gravity to move you sideways. Compare this way of covering the same distance with cross steps, leaping, hopping, etc. to find out for yourself which movement offers you the best speed and control.

Natural Steps Back and Forth

In your daily life, except when deliberately taking a Natural Stance, you are likely to find one foot to be further forward than the other. To take a Natural Step forward, simply lift your front foot off the ground without shifting your weight back and allow the force of gravity to move you forward. Trust your *quads*, the thigh muscles, which are usually the largest and strongest muscle group in the human body, to absorb the shock of landing. The muscles of the shins and calves are never as strong as the *quads*; therefore, landing on your heel or toes offers less shock absorption than landing on the flat foot and using your entire leg to soften your landing. Keeping your front knee sufficiently bent will enable you to land softly on the entire surface of the sole of the foot. Half-jokingly, I call it a "soleful step."

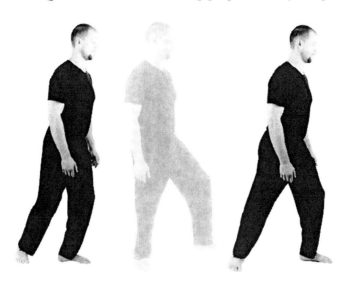

Taking a Natural Step forward

Another way to practice this type of step is by alternating the leading foot. There is a clever way to maneuver along a zigzag line as if you are a boat tacking against the wind. In order to avoid making cross steps, add a brief tap with the ball of the foot that you are moving forward from behind. You may choose to practice just tapping alone by imagining your lower leg to be a basketball that you can dribble with the same-side hand. This will help you develop an ability to bounce off the ground with the ball of the foot using the springiness of the calf muscles. This tapping motion is indispensable, for it allows you to receive a jolt of the energy of the element of Earth and send it through your body, which will prove quite useful in many Qi Dao applications.

To retreat, lift your back foot without shifting your weight onto the front one. Gravity will naturally propel you backward, so you will need to place your back foot on the ground before you land on your rear end. Apply the same method of absorbing the shock of landing as in the Natural Step forward. For instance, if the right foot is initially ahead of the left, step backward with the left foot turning the whole body slightly to the left. Immediately bring the front foot closer to the back one in order to avoid "spreading yourself too thin," as I put it.

Taking a Natural Step backward

You can develop gracefulness and speed in your movements by stepping back and forth with a tap between the steps. Right after stepping back with the left foot, tap with the ball of the right foot next to left and use the rebound from the ground to step forward with the right foot. After making the forward step, use the same tapping technique with the left foot to launch an immediate step backward. Continue bouncing back and forth until you feel confident in your movements and then reverse the positions of the feet.

In addition to that, practice multiple steps in one direction keeping the same foot ahead of the other, making sure you alternate which foot is leading from time to time. This way of performing Natural Step is an extremely swift way to move. Indeed, you may notice that it resembles the steps used in fencing, and naturally so, since fencing was once a discipline where moving swiftly was literally a matter of life and death. Those fencers who used cross steps instead of Natural Steps simply could not survive. As a result of that, their poor culture of movement was not perpetuated through the generations of their students, in contrast with the long lineage of Qi Dao adventurers.

Natural Turn

Natural Turn is similar to Natural Step in terms of moving the same side foot as the direction that you turn in. When performing Natural Turns, you either give your body circular momentum or you use the momentum you receive from being pushed by another person. Using such momentum, you can lift the appropriate foot and allow your body to turn in that respective direction, pivoting on the heel of the opposite foot. For instance, if you want to turn to the right, pick up the right foot and turn on the left heel. Explore the difference between the degrees of stability you experience when turning on the heel of the back foot versus the toes and feel which way of turning gives you a greater connection with Mother Earth.

Making a 180° Natural Turn

Natural Turn provides a way to turn around or just a few degrees, whatever necessary, in the shortest amount of time and with the least expenditure of energy. If you compare it to any other way of turning around, you will discover for yourself what many Qi Dao practitioners have practiced for millennia: if you need to turn 180 degrees, just lift the back foot and turn in the same direction as the name of that foot.

Energy Awareness

Qi Dao teaches that **energy is the inner essence of all things and events in this universe**. For example, pushing forward doesn't merely have something to do with projecting energy forward – it is a forward flow of energy. By exploring Harmonious Culture of Movement, you are not just preparing yourself for developing Energy Awareness, you are developing it!

The following principles of energy awareness involve alignment of the body while acting energetically in one direction or another. As your practice progresses, you will also learn to apply these principles in many aspects of life, such as dealing with energy projections from other people. In your travels, you may put these principles to test by engaging people from different cultures and backgrounds to participate in your experiments. I can guarantee that, as long as you coach them in an open-minded and non-dogmatic manner, most volunteers will come away from such experiments with a renewed sense of energy appreciation and grateful for your coaching. Of course, advanced Qi Dao students go through an apprenticeship program specifically dedicated to becoming particularly effective as Qigong coaches, but you may take some basic steps on your own if you feel so inclined. **Sharing your knowledge with others is a proven way to deepen your own knowledge**.

Orientation

Orienting by aligning the hand and the Centerline

The energy field of the human body projects a very powerful beam of focused attention forward. This beam lies in the *mid-sagittal* plane, the area directly in front of you, also known as Centerline. To find your Centerline, bring both hands together and draw a vertical line with your hands all the way up and down while in Natural Stance. Everything on that Centerline can receive your maximum attention (and you know by now that, on the basic level, **"energy flows wherever awareness, or attention, goes"**). Therefore, you can have the greatest degree of power and control over anything you deal with directly in front of you.

Compare using a heavy hammer with one hand on your Centerline versus slightly off center on either side. The further off center your hand goes, the more difficult, strained, and stressful the job becomes. The more the hand is aligned with your Centerline, the more precise and effortless your movements will be. This applies not only to hammering things but to virtually everything you deal with in life. For example, just imagine what it would be like to drive a car if the steering wheel was slightly to the side instead of being in front of you!

To find out about the Orientation of the human body, ask your partner to stand at your side and push your shoulder from the side. Make a mental note of the amount of effort it takes your partner to push you off balance.

Next, repeat this while turning your face towards your partner at the moment of the push. Notice whether it takes any more effort to push you off balance in this case. Then repeat the test once again but turn your whole body with a Natural Turn, pointing your navel at your partner at the moment of the push. Once again, notice whether it takes any more effort to push you off balance. The point of this test is to discover the power that your body gains when you use Orientation – awareness of your Centerline. It is not enough to just turn the head to face a challenge; the whole body must be involved in the process. Since you are learning not to be stuck in your head, this should give you another motivation to learn to pay attention to the whole body rather than just the head.

You can apply this principle of Orientation in different spheres of your life. Some things, like your computer screen and keyboard, the books you read or hand tools, can be used more efficiently when they are in alignment with your Centerline. In most cases, you can find a way to Orient yourself towards the things you deal with.

This principle applies to everything from lifting heavy things to dealing with people on the energetic level. If you have a boss or any authority figure trying to exercise control over you in certain situations, he or she will have less power over you if you move away from his or her Centerline while still keeping yourself Oriented towards that person. This will allow you to be less susceptible to being manipulated or bossed around. On the other hand, if you want to convey a message to people and make sure that they get it; make a point of orienting your Centerline towards them as they face you. This applies not only to external relationship issues, but also to inner processes such as fears, phobias, etc. Psychologically, **you can deal with various issues efficiently only when you face them directly**.

Stabilization

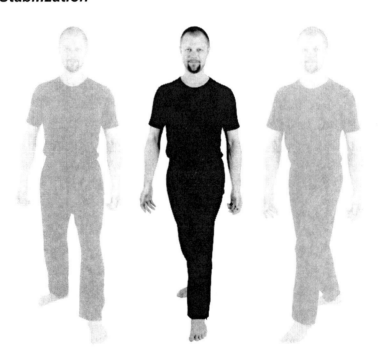

Exploring the Centerline alignment for Stabilization

Energetic empowerment associated with the Centerline alignment applies to the legs, too. Some Tai Chi enthusiasts develop a peculiar tendency to keep their weight on the back foot while facing forward. This inevitably makes them less stable than they could be if they only followed the principle of Stabilization. This principle is about turning the Centerline in the direction of the kneecap and toes of the weight-bearing leg. Try squatting or lunging while shifting most of your weight on one leg or the other. Pay attention to the amount of effort required for supporting your body with and without aligning your Centerline with the weight-bearing leg. Notice the amount of strength the weight-bearing leg has with and without Stabilization. The deeper your stance is the more obvious the difference will be.

To experience more benefits of Stabilization, ask your partner to test your stability with and without this alignment. First, shift your weight on one foot and turn your navel towards the same direction, with your partner pushing you from different sides. Second, turn your navel away from that foot and test again. Compare your sense of stability in both cases. Then repeat this test shifting on the other side to get the full picture.

You may even test this principle while standing on one foot. For better balance, make sure that you also observe the principle of Grounding.

Grounding

Experimenting with Grounding

Many schools of thought tend to talk about grounding in a metaphorical fashion. In Qi Dao, our method of Grounding is very concrete. Grounding is the method of keeping a strong energetic connection with Mother Earth when standing on your feet. It involves keeping the weight of the body over the centers of the feet, so that all edges of the feet apply equal pressure on the ground.

It may be helpful to imagine your foot as a suction cup. When the suction cup is not flat on a surface, it will not adhere easily to that surface. Similarly, the foot will not have much connection to the ground if the weight is distributed on its toes, heel, or on the inner or outer edge of the foot. The center of the suction cup is the point where the vacuum is created. The center of the foot is also the point of energetic connection with the ground. This is true, regardless of the fact that it may not touch the ground due to the arch of the foot.

Test your stability and balance with and without following the principle of Grounding. Just as in the test for alignment of the legs, you can learn to rely on the sensitivity of your feet to secure your balance. Remember the feelings you have in each case; compare them and choose the way that works best for you.

Rooting

The principle of Rooting is essential for maintaining balance and stability when projecting energy forward, especially when you are testing your practice partner. When you trade roles with your partner, it will be your turn to push him or her around. Being well Rooted will enable you to produce a consistent and effortless energy projection every time (this may sound really funny if you are familiar with the Australian slang… if that is the case, please pardon my language).

Generally speaking, your Root is the heel of the foot that is on the same side of the body as the hand or elbow you are pushing with. Experiment to find out whether it should be the front or the back foot when you push forward. It is interesting to note that most people unfamiliar with our Harmonious Culture of Movement tend to push with the front hand – the hand on the same side of the body as the front foot. It may be based on an unconscious idea that pushing is about pushing away something or someone in order to create greater distance rather than to project *Qi*. If you try to push another person away from you, you may be compelled to push with the front hand – the one on the same side of the body as the front foot. Compare the amount of strength in your front hand with the strength of the back hand – the hand on the side of the foot positioned further back.

Baseline alignment for better Rooting

Rooting requires keeping the back heel on the ground right on the Baseline, which is a straight line extending from the toes through the heel of the opposite foot towards the back foot. Test your stability and balance with and without such alignment. To make this test more dramatic, try to elevate the heel that serves as your Root when pushing your partner and then place it back on the ground. Remember the feelings you have in each case; compare them and choose your personal preference.

Centering

Many people wish to be more Centered in their daily lives, but have no specific methods to accomplish that. They often have only vague ideas about where the Center is; it may be quite difficult to become Centered without being aware of its location. The Center of your body is the line extending from the *Bai Hui* point on the top of your head, down the spine, all the way to the *Hui Yin* point on your perineum (the pressure point between your genitals and anus). In Oriental Medicine, it is called Central Channel and often referred to as the "Tai Chi Pole."

You can experience Centering by pivoting about 180 degrees on the heels, lifting the toes of one foot at a time and allowing your arms to swing freely so they touch the opposite hips as you pivot side to side. Breathe naturally, allowing the breath to synchronize with the movements of your body. Once you have established awareness of the Center of your body, you may notice that your breath becomes deeper and smoother, due to the relaxation of the muscles of your *abs* and *diaphragm*. Bring one hundred percent of your attention to the axis of your body, around which it pivots. Notice whether you are following the principle of Stabilization by tracking the direction of your Centerline with your weight-bearing foot. Test and compare your stability when pivoting around your spine versus any other way of pivoting.

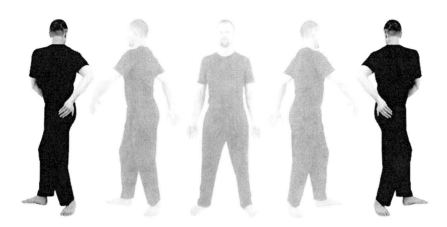

Finding the Center by pivoting

Being Centered allows you to delegate any energy projections coming at you to your Center. To test this, ask your partner to push you continuously into your stomach. From the point of view of statistics, it is very unlikely that your partner will be able to distribute an absolutely even amount of pressure on both sides of your Centerline. There is always going to be some more energy flowing to the right or to the left. Your task is to feel the side that receives more energy from the push and effortlessly pivot in that direction. If you really feel that your partner has found your Center precisely, which is statistically almost impossible, you may exercise your freedom of choice as to which way to turn.

Of course, energy projections are not always so tangible and easy to perceive. In your daily life, you may feel others projecting their emotions or attitudes towards you, perhaps eliciting a noticeable amount of reaction from you. By definition, reaction is a projection of energy in equal amount and in the direction opposite the initial action. Reacting to other people's energies is likely to escalate conflicts and produce more drama. If you do not like turning your life into a nightmare, **learning to be Centered will empower you to switch from reacting to responding to the flow of energies coming at you from others**. Responding means ability to sense the flow of oncoming energy and allowing your Center, the core of your Being, to take charge of the issue. With practice, you will be able to translate this principle from crude physical energy projections to emotional and psychological projections in every sphere of your life.

Lama Somananda Tantrapa

Chapter Three: Exploration of

Harmonious Culture of Movement

As with any culture, our Harmonious Culture of Movement needs more than one participant in order to have functionality and perpetuity. The growing tribe of Qi Dao practitioners is the best proof of its efficacy and guarantee of its survival. Similar to the belief of His Holiness, the Dalai Lama XIV, that the Chinese occupation of Tibet may be perceived as a blessing in disguise that facilitated spreading of the Tibetan spiritual wisdom all over the world, I believe that the worldwide transmission of Qi Dao will ensure its perpetuity through many generations to come.

Qi Dao offers a unique system of practices that are suitable for people, who do not want to be stuck within four walls, who would rather spend more time traveling or exploring the great outdoors. Generations upon generations of Qi Dao practitioners have tested this system in the most challenging conditions in the world, from the tallest mountains of Tibet to the Siberian caves deep underground. I have personally pushed the envelope even further by expanding the range of this practice to the stratosphere above the North Pole when flying from Moscow to New York as I was leaving the old country for good. I even experimented with practicing Qi Dao while diving not too far from the Mariana Trench, thus expanding its practice into the depths of the Pacific Ocean.

Many years of personal observation and innovation demonstrated to me that the practice of Qi Dao is particularly suitable for travelers, hikers and outdoor adventurers although anyone can really benefit from it. Unlike most systems of exercise and wellness disciplines, this practice does not require any special equipment, clothing, environment, or music to practice to. You can enjoy it on your own or with your practice partner(s), as well as in larger groups when participating in Qi Dao workshops and retreats. If you happen to enjoy and resonate with the energies of like-minded people from our international Qi Dao tribe, you will surely notice that synergizing the energies of a large number of practitioners boosts everyone's awareness and enjoyment of our Harmonious Culture of Movement.

If you spend some time observing people unfamiliar with our Harmonious Culture of Movement, you may notice that they often move with linear, start-stop and jerky motions that require a lot of energy. Constantly stopping and restarting your movements can certainly consume more energy than continuous circular motion, because it usually takes just as much energy to stop a movement as it takes to initiate it. Any exercise routines that include disharmonious movements can easily deplete your energy resources and leave you exhausted and sore. Just imagine trying to travel across the country constantly starting and stalling your car!

In contrast to that, Qi Dao invites you to develop an alternative culture of movement that integrates your entire organism. Its Harmonious Culture of Movement is based on smooth, flowing, non-stop motions. Fluid and graceful, these motions are free of rigidity and stuckness. Instead of exercises using the isolation of certain muscles or parts of the body, it suggests to synergize the movements of the whole system in order to animate any particular part of the body. On the basic level of practice, Qi Dao teaches you to explore and enjoy your range of motion by sending waves of energy throughout your body radiating from the Center to the periphery of the organism – your limbs.

You can develop a tension-free culture of movement by opening to the flow of *Qi* any areas that used to be beyond your old comfort zone and by integrating them into your new identity. You will learn to transcend the limitations imposed by pain and discomfort by shifting your attitude towards those edges – shifting from perceiving them as obstacles to perceiving them as learning opportunities. With practice, you will find yourself enjoying more and more freedom each time you view your limitations as temporary phases of the journey dedicated to living your dreams.

Harmonious Culture of Movement is dedicated to creating a new, more natural energy dynamic in your body, empowering you to experience the fluidity of movement and freedom of expression associated with being in the flow. When you are in the flow, you can be balanced and relaxed, all life challenges notwithstanding. Since this is not an exercise routine but a whole new culture of movement, it systematically approaches every aspect of life. It facilitates being in the flow not just once in a blue moon, but regularly throughout your daily life (e.g., working, healing, fighting, lovemaking, meditating, walking in the park, sleeping and dreaming).

Range of Motion Exploration

Begin these explorations slowly and gently. First, find the center of your comfort zone, the most comfortable and Neutral state of alignment. Second, explore the extent of the comfort zone by experimenting with your range of motion, degrees of tension or amount of pressure. Third, explore the edges of your comfort zone. There is no need to push yourself over the edge of the comfort zone by forcing your body beyond what it is currently capable of. Just being present at the edge of your comfort zone for a while will allow you to expand it. Finally, **find your authentic ways to manifest your dreams and aspirations that usually reside beyond the edges of your comfort zone.**

If you pay attention to your breath during the exploration of your Culture of Movement, you may learn about the natural synchronization of your breathing with the rhythm of your movements. Take Torso Rotation as an example: many beginners appear to be confused as to the most natural timing for exhaling and inhaling during the rotation of the torso. This confusion must have something to do with misconceptions regarding the mechanism of *respiration* in general.

How would you answer a question whether your *diaphragm* (the breathing muscle) should contract or relax when you breathe out? Surprisingly, even health professionals, including physicians, nurses, physical therapists, etc., often admit that they think the *diaphragm* is supposed to contract on exhalation. This must explain the excessive degrees of tension in their bodies resulting from trying to contract the muscle that they actually need to relax in order to breathe naturally. I invite you to free yourself from any attempts to breathe "correctly." Being natural –

one of our foundational principles – is more essential than the number of repetitions, form or speed of movements when practicing Qi Dao. After all, **what could possibly be healthier for you than being natural?**

Speaking of repetitions, you will not need to do more than a few repetitions of each type of movement to thoroughly explore your range of motion. Although the following exploration of the range of motion is presented in the order given below, it is not a set regimen to follow, other than beginning with Natural Stance. If some part of your body requires attention first, give it the attention it needs. Stay free from routines; enjoy mixing some spontaneity into your practice and go with the flow.

Head Rotations

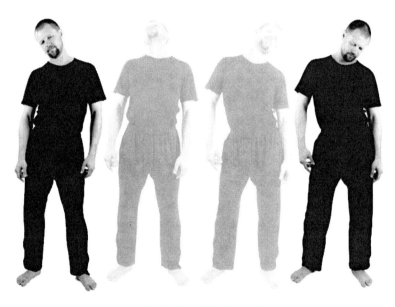

Rotating the head

First of all, assume your Natural Stance. Begin exploring the mobility of your neck by rotating your pelvis in a circular manner clockwise and counter-clockwise. Allow the motions of the torso to animate the head letting the head roll freely, in synch with the motions of the pelvis without using the neck muscles. Use the principle of Grounding to maintain your balance while keeping your whole torso relaxed throughout the movement and letting your arms hang loose and aligned at your sides.

You may find some muscles around your neck that are sore or tense, which often contributes to the energetic disconnect between the head and the rest of the body. If you find it challenging to synchronize the movements of your Upper *Dan Tien* (the energy center in the head) and Lower *Dan Tien* (the energy center in the pelvis), this may indicate general lack of communication between the head and the rest of your body. When this is the case, most people usually do not get stuck in the body but rather in the head. If you experience this kind of challenge, bring attention to the areas of tension in your neck or along the spine to empower and relax those parts of your body using the methods described in the section dedicated to the alignment of the head. When you bring your attention there, you will soon notice some changes happening in those muscles.

Shoulder Rolls

Rolling both shoulders together

Explore the mobility of your shoulders and their connection with the lower body. Roll both shoulders forward, using the undulation of your pelvis to send a wave up your spine that moves the shoulders. After a few repetitions, reverse the motion and roll both shoulders backwards still keeping your arms relaxed at your sides. Notice that this backwards motion is similar to rowing a boat, less the movements of the arms. Naturally, rowing a boat requires a continuous expenditure of energy, and rowers have to use the muscles of the entire body. If rowers only used their *trapezius* muscles, they would quickly tire.

Rolling the shoulders following each other

Now roll your shoulders one following the other forward. Let them accomplish this motion without any muscular effort by merely shifting your weight from side to side and rocking the hips alternately up and down. Reverse the movement and roll the shoulders one following the other backwards. This is an excellent exercise for the muscles of the upper back, because they get engaged in the movement without having to tense up. In fact, if they are tense, they will prevent the waves from flowing from the pelvis into your shoulders, but these shoulder rolls can also loosen up the tense muscles.

Arms Rotations

Rotating both arms together

Resume your Natural Stance once again and swing your arms back and forth loosely by undulating your pelvis. Keep your shoulder muscles totally relaxed. Imagine your arms to be ropes attached to your shoulders, animated only by the motions of your torso. Explore your ability to rotate both arms forward and – after several revolutions – backwards in a windmill motion using a wave flowing from the pelvis up the spine into the arms. The shoulder muscles should not get tired doing this as long as you are not using them to rotate the arms.

Another interesting experiment you can do here is about *pronation* and *supination* of the arms. You will likely notice that if you turn your palms backwards, it is hardly possible to rotate the arms fully around your shoulders. Pay attention to the flow of energy in your arms and compare the feelings before and after this exploration. If you wish to have more energy available in the hands for your creative endeavors, give particular attention to the ways you can keep your arms and shoulders relaxed.

Rotating the arms in the opposite directions

Now let us find out whether you can rotate your arms in the opposite directions at the same time: one arm forward and the other one backwards. These arm rotations can be easier when you allow the hips to pivot. Whenever you are ready, reverse the directions of these arm rotations. This is an excellent exercise for developing greater coordination between the two hemispheres of the brain.

Opening and Closing

Opening and closing both arms simultaneously

Open and close both arms simultaneously while alternating the arm that is on top when closing. When opening the arms, remember to turn the palms of both hands upwards on your shoulder level. Allow your breath to naturally synchronize with the motions of the arms and torso. Discover for yourself the way to make opening and closing following a trajection similar to the sign of infinity – just like a digit eight but sideways.

Experiment with modifying the basic Centering exercise that involves pivoting the whole body and swinging the arms left and right. Turn your whole body left and right around its vertical axis pivoting on your heels, one foot at a time, and keeping just a little over 50% of your weight on the front foot. Glance at the hand going behind your back to see how you can keep it at shoulder level, palm facing upward.

Since your *cervical* spine is a part of the entire spine, allow it to continue the torque of the rest of your spine when performing this movement. Compare it with turning your head in the opposite direction and feel how that affects the flow of this movement.

Opening and closing alternating arms

Please make a note about the names of these movements. You will find them used quite frequently throughout this and more advanced Qi Dao materials. Although Closing in this exercise is identical to the Closing with an elbow that you will be learning soon, this particular type of Opening is slightly different, yet similar enough to warrant the same name. For example, this is the only time when you will be prompted *supinate* your hand (turn the palm upward) when practicing Opening.

Torso Rotations

Torso rotation with the arms behind the back

Making sure that you are in your Natural Stance, explore the range of motion of your shoulders by bringing your hands towards each other behind your back reaching over with one arm over your head and the other one down and around your torso. If you have any difficulty grasping the fingers behind your back this way, use a stick to inch your hands towards each other till you reach the limit of your range of motion. See if you can keep your body mass Centered by distributing equal weight on each foot. It can be useful to imagine that you are doing this exercise on ice, or any slippery surface, where it is crucial to maintain your balance.

When you are ready, alternate the positions of the arms and reverse the direction of rotation. Notice whether one of your shoulders is tighter than the other, thus calling for more attention. In many cases, pain in the shoulder muscles (especially *anterior deltoid*) can be attributed to the excessive *pronation* of the arm, which often contributes to energy deficiency in the arm and hand.

Torso rotation with the arms in front

Next, bring one elbow on top of the other and wrap your forearms around each other until the fingers of the lower hand touch the palm of the other hand, thumbs facing you. Add the rotation of your entire upper body in a circular fashion around your waist, letting your head roll around freely. After a few circles, alternate the arms and reverse the torso rotation. Again, it is particularly essential to keep your weight Centered between your feet to maintain balance.

Leg Rotations

Outward rotation of the leg bent at the knee

Experiment with standing on the left foot and rotating the right leg bent at the knee clockwise (outwards) in a circular manner in front of you. Allow your leg to hang loose and free of any muscular tension to experience the full range of movement in your hip joint. If you choose to speed up, you may find that centrifugal force of the leg rotation will cause the foot to rise up to the level of the knee. After a few revolutions, alternate the legs and explore the same type of movement on the other side.

Inward rotation of the leg bent at the knee

Now rotate the right leg bent in the knee counter-clockwise in a circular fashion in front of you. Allow your hips to open fully when your knee comes up and close them as your knee comes down. See if you can keep your torso and head aligned while making smooth circles with the knee. When you are ready to switch sides, explore the same movement with the left leg.

As an alternative, you may choose to rotate one leg in one direction after the other and then do the same with the other leg. Compare the feelings of the flow in your legs and feet before and after this exploration to find out for yourself what you can do to facilitate free flow of energy in your hips and legs. Developing coordination and balance will also contribute to an unobstructed flow of *Qi* in your legs.

Knee Rotations

Rotating the knees

Standing with both feet together, knees slightly bent, place your hands on the kneecaps and rotate the knees in circles in one direction and then the other. Sometimes, your may find your *hamstrings* or other leg muscles tenser that you wish they were. Exploring the range of movement of your knees may help you discover any areas of tension that you may have around your knees. Most of the muscles of the leg are attached to the bones of the lower leg around the knee joint and can create pain below the knee when chronically tense. As long as the knee pain is caused by a tense muscle, rather than a torn *meniscus*, you can easily heal yourself by exploring your range of motion and flexibility (see the next subchapter).

Well, I have to admit that self-healing is simple but may not be easy at first; however, rest assured that it will become easier and more natural with practice. Take your time to develop a greater appreciation of the flow of *Qi* around your knees, which are among the most complex and frequently abused joints in the human body. This exploration is also useful for learning to distinguish the action of bending at the hips from bending at the waist while maintaining the alignment of the torso.

Ankle Rotations

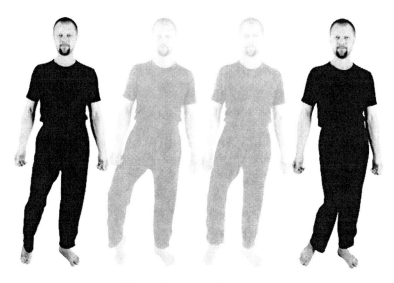

Rotating the right ankle

Explore the flexibility of your ankles, one at a time, by lifting the heel of one foot off the ground and rotating it in a circular motion. Make these circles clockwise and counter-clockwise using the whole leg and hip to rotate the ankle around the ball of the foot. After a few revolutions, do the same experiment with the other foot.

Compare perceptions of energy flow in the feet before you switch feet and do the same on the other side. Similar to the rotation of the head, with which you started your exploration of Harmonious Culture of Movement, these ankle rotations help develop a better energetic connection with your feet. You may feel very different when rotating your ankles with the motion of the whole legs versus isolating them and rotating the feet by themselves. Enjoy a more harmonious relationship with Mother Earth that you will undoubtedly discover to be a positive side-effect of your experimentation.

Flexibility Exploration

Greater flexibility and range of motion often promote a greater sense of comfort and freedom in movement. The degree of physical mobility is usually indicative of mental lucidity or lack thereof. Since everything is interconnected in the human being, you cannot attain mental flexibility without addressing physical flexibility and vice versa. Can you claim to be a relaxed person if you hold tension in your body?

Paradoxically, many people associate stretching with greater flexibility. There are various popular methods and programs promising improvement of flexibility through stretching. First of all, when exploring your flexibility, bear in mind that Qi Dao does not teach you to stretch your muscles or other tissues. When temporarily stretched, the muscles will act almost like rubber bands, tightening up as soon as they are allowed to. This is called "stretch reflex." It challenges many athletes, martial artists and Yoga enthusiasts puzzled by the inadequate results of their stretching exercises despite their formidable efforts to improve flexibility. Instead of stretching, Qi Dao suggests lengthening your muscles. Literally opposite to the way stretching works, lengthening involves shortening the muscle and making it tired of being short before allowing it to lengthen thereby expanding the range of motion and flexibility.

At this point, let's take a brief excursion into one of the finer principles of Qi Dao practice in order to establish the groundwork for the following investigation of lengthening. Imagine for a moment a muscle that you would like to make more flexible. It may remind you of a rubber band – elastic and resilient. Some muscles may be stretchier, others are stiffer. What response can you expect from an inflexible tissue if you start to pull it by the opposite ends? Not unlike the rubber band, it will most likely rebound and shorten after being forcefully stretched – this is stretch reflex in action. The more you try to pull the poor muscle, the stronger it will fight against such a heavy-handed approach. This should shed light on the meager, if not disappointing progress of those who try to improve flexibility using stretching. This example should also suggest an alternative, less invasive way to work with tense muscles. If you have been doing something that did not bring you the desirable results, consider doing something different.

Imagine being able to communicate with the muscle so that it can tell you how it feels and what it wants. If it is sore and tense, maybe it is trying to tell you that it wants to experience something, perhaps, being shorter? With all due respect, you may have to oblige and assist that part of yourself in manifesting its dream, whatever it may be. In fact, you may regard your entire being as a sum total of different parts that are constantly dreaming of something.

This may remind you of interpersonal relationships. The more you help others in manifesting their dreams, the more they will assist you in manifesting yours. Similarly, **the more you assist your muscles, organs and other parts of your organism in manifesting their dreams, the more they will support you in manifesting yours**. Besides, would it not just feel great to enjoy being in a happy and healthy body?

How can you help a tense muscle manifest its dream? You may start by measuring the level of well-being of that body part. Subjectively assess it on the scale from zero to one hundred, where the top of the scale equals a 100% healthy state. It is crucial to measure well-being rather than pain or suffering, because your consciousness will begin creating pictures of the condition you are measuring thus promoting that condition.

If the part of your body in question is at 60% level of well-being due to tension, explore your ability to change it, say to 50%, by tensing it up a little more. That is right, instead of forcing it to relax or subjecting it to stretching; you are letting it do what it wants to do at the moment – tense up.

If you have any chronic tension, you may not really know how tense you are until you experiment with tensing up more and then releasing extra tension. Sometimes the habit of tension is so ingrained in the autonomous nervous system that you may think you are relaxed when you are actually holding tension, which exemplifies miscommunication. You can start reconnecting with various parts of yourself that you want to reconnect with by sending commands to increase tension. You will almost immediately receive feedback – signals of greater discomfort and/or pain – reporting that attention is needed there.

The first difference between stretching and lengthening is in the initial action. Stretching begins with pulling the opposite ends of the muscle apart from each other, while lengthening begins with making it shorter. When the muscle is allowed to shorten, with or without tensing up more, its first response may be bewilderment. If it could speak it might say, "Do you truly mean it? Will you really let me shorten instead of stretching me against my resistance?" Your muscle will soon recognize that it does not have to be tense to feel better. When your central nervous system realizes that it no longer has to be tense, it will start letting go. Interestingly enough, as soon as you stop sending signals of tension, it will be able to become more relaxed than it used to be, at the same time lengthening naturally.

As soon as lengthening begins, it may induce a sigh of release, which would indicate to a skilled Qi Dao practitioner that the body-mind is ready to let go of the internal issues that were causing the external tension. As you pay attention to your own body language through touch and movement, you will notice that your whole body-mind responds much more favorably to lengthening of your muscles than stretching them. After a few repetitions of this maneuver, I suggest to assess your level of wellness once again. Most likely, you will find this particular part of the body resonating with 70% of well-being, if not even higher, which will naturally translate into greater relaxation and flexibility.

Calves

Exploring the flexibility of the right calf

Place one foot in front of the other, both feet facing forward, parallel to each other. Explore the flexibility of the calf muscles by shifting your weight back and forth. Contract the calves as you lift the back heel off the ground, and then relax them as you drop the heel back on the ground. You can find out more about the edge of your comfort zone by standing in front of a wall and pushing into it with both hands while lifting your back heel and bringing it back to the ground in synch with your breathing. Remember that it is usually easier to lengthen the muscles that are tired after receiving a workout. After several repetitions, alternate the legs.

Shins

Exploring the flexibility of the left shin

Investigate the flexibility of the muscles of your shins by alternately balancing on one leg and placing the top of the opposite foot on the floor behind you. Keeping both knees slightly bent, rock the back foot gently from side to side to discover its range of motion and explore the edge of your comfort zone. Rather than harassing your shins by stretching them, let them lengthen as you imagine that you can breathe through them. Switch to the other foot after a few repetitions.

Thighs

Exploring the flexibility of the thighs standing

Lift one leg, bent at the knee, behind you and use both hands to hold onto the foot. Raise the foot as high in the air as possible, bending forward at the hips to maintain balance and alignment. Explore the same move switching to the other foot. Remember that the *quadriceps* form the largest muscle group in the body. You will do yourself a great favor by facilitating lengthening and relaxation of your *quads*. Their muscles-antagonists are *hamstrings*, which you may notice lengthening in the standing leg as you tilt the upper body forward lifting the foot behind you. This will promote the flow of *Qi* in your legs and enhance their strength and mobility. Alternate legs whenever you are ready.

Exploring the flexibility of the thighs on the ground

If you feel adventurous enough, you may experiment with another, more challenging exploration of the flexibility of your thighs and *hip flexors*, which include *rectus femoris, ilio-psoas* and *sartorius*. Kneel on the floor keeping about one foot distance both between your knees and feet, so that you can fit your hips between the feet. Reach for the floor behind you and start walking your hands backward, tilting your torso as far back as you can. Initially, go only as far as you feel appropriate. As your flexibility increases, you may find you are able to lay your back flat on the floor behind you. Continue to breathe naturally throughout your explorations.

Hips

Exploring the flexibility of the hips standing

Begin your exploration of the flexibility of your hips by resuming a Natural Stance. Standing upright, raise your left knee and hug it with the right arm, so that the left elbow goes around the left knee. As you straighten your back, check how closely you can bring the right knee toward the left shoulder without loosing balance. Check whether bringing your center of weight over the center of the standing foot gives you maximum stability. In synch with your breath, contract and relax the right *gluteus* (buttocks muscles) to help them release any excessive tension. When you feel like switching sides, continue your exploration with the other leg.

Exploring the flexibility of the hips on the ground

As with the previous exercise, you may opt to conduct this exploration on the floor. Sitting on the floor, bend your right leg in front of your body with the left leg fully extended behind you. Position the right foot so that it extends slightly to the left of your left hip. Begin by contracting your *gluteus* and *periformis* (the *hip extensor* beneath the *gluteus*) as you inhale and relaxing as you exhale. Then explore the flexibility of your hips by bending forward in the hip socket and rocking from side to side imagining your breath flowing through the right hip joint. You may also experiment with the left *hip flexors* by angling your upper body as straight upwards as you can and moving it up and down a few times. Before you alternate the legs, notice if there is any difference in flexibility between the two sides. If so, give some extra attention to the side that holds more tension.

Adductors

Exploring the flexibility of the *adductors* with splits

Explore how far you can put your feet apart as if you are going to perform a side split. Discover whether you can bend forward and allow your elbows to reach the floor by walking your right hand to the left and your left hand to the right past each other. You can tense up and relax the *adductors* and *gracilis*, the muscles of your inner thighs, while imagining that you can breathe through those muscles. In order to explore the flexibility of these muscles, rock back and forth shifting the weight from the heels to the elbows and back to the heels in synch with your breath. This part of your body may be particularly resistant to stretching, so please exercise caution while experimenting with the splits. You will enjoy most improvement if you maintain keen awareness of the limitations of your comfort zone and take time to allow the muscles to let go of habitual tension.

Hamstrings

Exploring the flexibility of the *hamstrings* with splits

Keeping your feet wide apart, turn your hips to the right as you walk your hands in that direction, so that the right hand ends up on the right side of the right leg. Explore the flexibility of your *hamstrings* by rocking from one hand to the other. Alternate the legs by walking the hands to the opposite side. Make sure you point the toes of your front foot upward while keeping the front knee as straight as you can.

After returning to the standing side-split position, find out whether you can sit down without moving your feet any closer to each other by simply walking your hands backward, palms on the floor and fingers pointing backward. After you land softly on your buttocks (initially, you may opt for a pillow strategically placed under your rear end), explore how far you can bend forward and reach with your fingers while keeping your back as straight as possible. Notice your breathing without forcing your breath, and allow the relaxation that comes with each exhale to bring your torso further forward.

Exploring the flexibility of the *hamstrings* in motion

Once you've reached the edge of your comfort zone, walk your hands to one side and reach for the respective foot with both hands. Rock the whole body from side to side revolving the entire leg so that the foot turns from eleven o'clock to one o'clock and back in synch with breathing. Then walk your hands to the other side and reach for the opposite foot to explore the flexibility of the *hamstrings* of that leg. Continue your exploration by rocking side to side and turning the other leg in a similar manner. Then walk your hands forward again to see if you are more flexible after just a few minutes of exploring this practice. I hope you understand that any **substantial improvement can only be experienced when you make this practice a regular part of your daily life.**

Obliques

Exploring the flexibility of the *obliques* on the ground

Now, let's explore the flexibility of your *obliques* (side muscles). Sitting with your legs spread wide apart, bring your left foot toward your crotch and bend the whole torso to the opposite side, reaching with the left hand over your head for the right foot, elbow pointing up. If you feel like you need more challenge, you may hold onto the left knee with your right hand while bending to the right. Following the rhythm of your breath, rock the whole body back and forth while turning the entire leg so that the foot rotates between eleven o'clock and one o'clock. Alternate the legs by pulling the right foot toward your crotch and straightening the left one, reaching for the left foot with the opposite hand. For greater relaxation of the *obliques*, add the imagery of your breath flowing in and out of your body through a point on the side at the end of the twelfth rib.

Groin

Exploring the flexibility of the groin on the ground

This exploration may remind you of a popular "butterfly" exercise although with lengthening rather than stretching in mind. Sitting on the floor with legs bent and the soles of both touching each other, hold the feet with both hands as close to your crotch as possible. Gently apply some pressure on your inner thighs with your elbows while leaning forward and exhaling. Lower your head towards the feet keeping your back as straight as possible. Inhale when you come back up contracting the *pectineus* (groin muscles). You can rock back and forth like this, in synch with your breathing, until you experience letting go of any excessive tension and lengthening of the groin muscles. The main challenge is to move slowly instead of rapid and jerky motions of the legs up and down, hence the name "butterfly." You will notice a significant increase in flexibility if you practice these movements mindfully on a regular basis without overdoing them.

Wrist Rolls

Rolling the wrists

Interlock the fingers of both hands together and imagine holding a small ball of energy, about the size of a tennis ball. Explore rolling your hands around the energy ball in one direction (whichever you prefer). Then alternate the way your fingers interlock, so that the other thumb is on top, and reverse the direction of rotation. We often have habitual ways to interlock our fingers with one or the other thumb being always on top. Challenge your stereotypes by learning to interlock your fingers just as comfortably either way. If you pay particular attention to the energy flow in your hands during this and the following explorations, you may find your own way to keep your hands and wrists loose in order to promote the free flow of *Qi*.

Hand Pins

Exploring Hand Pin

Place the right hand in front of you with the palm facing you. Grasp the right wrist with the left pinky and ring fingers while placing your left thumb on the knuckle of the right pinky. Keeping the center of the left palm (*Lao Gong* point) on the back of the right hand, alternate tension and relaxation of the *pronators* of your right wrist while moving both hands up and down along the Centerline of your body. You will not need to use any special effort to move your hands, let the force of gravity do most of the work. Experiment with the flexibility of the wrist by pushing with the left thumb on the knuckles of other hand's fingers to find out which position challenges you the most. Imagine that you can breathe through your right arm as if it as if were a snorkel, thereby bringing energy and relaxation into the arm. Switch to the other hand after several repetitions of this movement.

Arm Bars

Exploring Arm Bar

Extend your right arm on the Centerline in front of you and turn the palm towards the right side, right thumb facing down. Grasp the back of the right hand with your left one placing the left thumb on the crease of the right wrist, left hand's *Lao Gong* point on the back of the right hand and the left hand's fingers on the knuckles of the left. Keeping your elbows level, experiment with contracting the *wrist extensors* of your right arm at the same time as you breathe in. Then relax as you push on the knuckles of the right hand towards the right elbow while breathing out. Continue exploring the flexibility of the muscles of your forearm by slowly bending both elbows while keeping pressure on the knuckles and then straightening the right arm in synch with your breathing. Use your imagination to make it easier to stay on the edge of your comfort zone, imagine that you can breathe through your arm as if through a hose that can be bent without creating a kink. Alternate your hands after a few motions back and forth.

Rotation of the Palms

Exploring the flexibility of the *wrist flexors*

Bring both hands together in front of you in a prayer like fashion (*Namaste* gesture for those of you who are familiar with Yoga). Slide the right hand upward about half an inch, so that the right fingers are about half an inch higher than the left fingers. To explore and enhance the flexibility of your left *wrist flexors*, contract and relax them and then gently push the fingers of the left hand (including the thumb) toward the left elbow far enough to find the edge of your comfort zone. Still keeping the hands in front of you slowly rotate the hands forward and down, then back up and inwards, allowing the muscles of the forearms to lengthen. Alternate hands whenever you are ready.

To complete each Qi Dao practice session spend a few minutes in quiet meditation either standing in *Zhan Zhuang* (Natural Stance), kneeling Zen-style in *Seiza* or relaxing on your back in *Savasana* (the Corpse Pose in Yoga). Try them out and follow your inner guidance to find which meditation position you resonate with best at the present moment. Bringing the hands together in a *Namaste* position and bowing to your coach or practice partner is a traditional expression of respect and appreciation of each other at the end of the practice session. One of the meanings of the Sanskrit word *Namaste* is **"the divine within me pays homage to the divine within you."**

Lama Somananda Tantrapa

Chapter Four: Six Directional Movements

Qi Dao respects the philosophical principles of *Yin* and *Yang* common in Oriental schools of thought, which oppose as well as complement and balance each other. Like a magnet where the positive and negative poles cannot exist without each other, *Yin* and *Yang* movements need to work together to balance and synchronize the body and its energy field. In each spatial plane of movement, such as the *mid-sagittal* (Centerline), *frontal* (vertical) and *transverse* (horizontal) planes, there are directions having *Yin* or *Yang* qualities.

Yin movements represent the feminine aspect of universal energy flowing forward, downward and inward, each viewed in relation to one's center. *Yang* movements represent the masculine aspect of universal energy flowing backward, upward and outward, again viewed in relation to one's center. It is interesting to note that Western medical terminology uses the identical categories of direction: *anterior* – forward, *inferior* – downward, *interior* – inward, *posterior* – backward, *exterior* – outward and *superior* – upward.

The basic directional movements of Qi Dao are paired up in each of the spatial dimensions. When one arm performs a primary movement, the opposite arm makes a secondary movement to provide counter-balance. By definition, primary movement is a movement that coincides with the direction of the motion of the body's center of mass. The power of the primary movement does not come from the tension of the arm muscles, but from the momentum of the whole body. Secondary movement is usually a movement of the opposite arm in reverse. Most secondary movements have no inherent power because they move in the direction opposite to the momentum of the body.

Forward Push, Closing and Downward Press in this context require *transverse* motion of the legs – stepping towards the target with the opposite foot from the arm making the primary movement and bringing the weight on the front foot. Backward Pull, Opening and Upper Cut, on the other hand, usually require *homolateral* motion of the legs – stepping towards the target with the foot on the same side of the body as the arm making the primary movement.

In your travels, you may find yourself in some tough situations when someone may be aggressive toward you or your company. Rest assured that Qi Dao is not only an enlightening energy art, but also a superb martial art. In this chapter, you will find some basic examples of self-defense application of the six directional movements that can help you free yourself from someone's grip. When someone grabs you by the hand or wrist, that person may either grab you with the hand on the same side of the body (Parallel Grip) or with the opposite hand across the Centerline (Cross Grip). You may find that any grip has strong and weak points.

The strongest point in any grip is in the center of the palm – *Lao Gong* acupuncture point. Imagine a vector of force emanating from the center of the palm perpendicular to its surface. This means that pushing against the palm of the grabbing hand would be going against the flow of the grip's energy. Going with the flow of that energy would require moving in the direction in which the other person's *Lao Gong* point is pointing. With practice, you will learn not only to detect the direction of that flow with your eyes closed but even to sense that direction before the opponent's hand reaches you.

Alternating roles with your adventure partner practice elbow strikes on small and light targets like foam-padded sticks regularly sold in martial arts supply stores (you will need those for your future practice, too, if you continue exploring more advanced applications of Qi Dao). The ideal dimensions of the stick are one-half of your height in length and about one inch in diameter. It should be padded for beginning training using foam or rubber tube that also slightly covers both ends of the stick. Holding one stick in each hand your practice partner can provide you with two targets to hone your precision and coordination. Hitting the stick with an elbow may not be very pleasant, so go slowly and do not try to hit too hard. One of the most ubiquitous habits developed by martial artists is trying to hit their targets harder and harder forgetting about awareness, timing and alignments. Imagine practicing these movements as if you are practicing Tai Chi – slowly and effortlessly. It will make your practice more meditative and pleasant. Qi Dao teaches that only harmonious steps can lead you to harmonious goals.

Forward Push

You can put the principles of the Harmonious Culture of Movement to the test while learning to create a powerful energy flow forward. You can start by figuring out which hand would be more effective to use for pushing forward. Compare making a push with your "front hand" versus pushing with your "back hand" (the hand opposite the front foot), as you step forward with the front foot. Through trial and error you will discover the way to utilize *transverse* movement of your body.

When your front foot lifts off the ground initiating your Natural Step, see if you can align your hips momentarily with the toes of the back foot, since it becomes your weight-bearing foot until the stepping foot lands. If your back foot does not become the weight-bearing one for a moment, you must be levitating!

Forward Push with the right elbow

Initially, Forward Push should be learned with an elbow rather than a hand, since pushing with an elbow requires no muscular tension in the arm. Instead of using physical force, you will learn to use the power of the element of Earth (gravity and the strength of your bones). Imagine a skeleton making an elbow strike. Such an imaginary strike would only have power if the elbow were on the Centerline, with the bones coming into alignment between the elbow and the back heel. Touching the opposite shoulder with the hand naturally brings the elbow to the Centerline. This follows the principle of Orientation, the first one of the four main principles in this method of energy projection.

The second principle is Stabilization, which involves the alignment of the Centerline with the toes and knee of the front leg stepping forward. As soon as the sole of the front foot lands on the ground, the leg will be able to easily absorb the shock with the muscles of the thighs if you keep that knee soft and bent just enough to cover the toes from your sight. If you try to use the muscles of your shins to absorb the shock of landing by reaching the ground with the heel first, it will require tension in your lower legs, preventing energetic connection with the ground. The same may happen when trying to use the calves by landing on the toes first, which is much less efficient than using the largest muscles of the body – *quadriceps* – to absorb the shock of landing.

The third principle is Rooting, which includes alignment of the back heel with the baseline. When finishing your Forward Push, see if you can draw a straight line from the toes of your front foot through the heel toward the heel of the back foot. This is your baseline. Test your stability and strength when the back heel is on the baseline versus when it is not. Whenever the back heel is not on the baseline, or is lifted off the ground, you will likely feel uprooted and only able to push yourself away from the target.

The fourth principle is Streamlining, which involves the alignment of the torso with the back leg. This is the key principle, since all of the previous principles will not be sufficient to produce a powerful Forward Push without this last one. When performing a Forward Push, observe the line from the top of your head down the spine and all the way down to the heel of the back leg creating a straight line as if someone has placed a board on your back. To test this principle, practice your Forward Push against your partner's resistance while keeping your entire body Streamlined. Now compare that by pushing while slightly deviating from the Streamlined position of the body by either keeping the torso too vertical or tilting it too far forward. Notice the difference in the power of your Forward Push with and without this key alignment.

Backward Pull

As the name implies, this is the reversal of Forward Push that can be used to project energy backward. You can employ it either to pull with the grip of the back hand or to strike with the back elbow. As one of the three *Yang* movements, Backward Pull requires making a Natural Step in the direction of your target with the foot on the same side of the body as the hand performing the primary movement. Lifting the back foot initiates the movement of the center of mass in that direction as the pelvis begins to turn in preparation for aligning with the back foot upon landing. The pulling hand needs to stay close to the body on your Centerline, palm turning upwards.

Backward Pull with the left elbow

Orientation is the first of the four main principles pertinent in projecting energy backwards. To test it, engage your practice partner in an improvised game of tug-of-war holding your stick with only one hand. Make a note that in this case, it is the hand, rather than the elbow, that needs to be in alignment with the Centerline.

Stabilization is the second principle used in Backward Pull. It is similar to the one in Forward Push in terms of the pelvis turning to align the Centerline with the weight-bearing foot. In Backward Pull, however, the weight shifts on the back leg rather than the front one. Therefore, the Centerline needs to align with the back foot in this movement. Ask your practice partner to test your stability when you follow this principle and when you do not. Draw your own conclusions from the results of your testing.

The third principle, Rooting, is about the alignment of the back heel with your baseline. In Backward Pull, the forearm involved in your primary movement also needs to be aligned with the baseline. To humor me, try deviating from this alignment and examine the outcome.

The fourth alignment, Streamlining, is also crucial in Backward Pull. Imagine a vertical plumb line dropping down from the top of your head. If your spine aligns with that straight line that continues down toward your back heel, you will have maximum strength and stability in your Backward Pull. Turning the head to see your target is imperative to ensure that you hit the right person behind you; maintaining the vertical alignment of the neck is essential in this maneuver. Imagine wearing a helmet that allows you to turn your head but prevents you from tilting it sideways at the same time. Compare practicing Backward Pull with and without this alignment to find the way of performing this movement that works best for you.

Applications:

Backward Pull – Forward Push

Backward Pull – Forward Push application

Ask your partner to grab your left hand with his or her left hand. This type of grip is called Cross Grip. Notice the direction of your partner's *Lao Gong* point on the grabbing hand. If it points behind you, this presents an opportunity to use a combination of Backward Pull and Forward Push. Begin with imitating Backward Pull, stepping with your back foot away from your partner's Centerline. Make sure that you do not use any force to move his or her hand from the position in space it is in; you just assume the position of the body as if you are making a Backward Pull while aligning your left forearm with your partner's forearm.

Aligning the forearms should then enable you to turn your palm downwards to get the "upper hand," literally placing your hand on top of your partner's. Only when you get the upper hand, will you be able to proceed with a Forward Push directed at your partner's head or throat. Without getting your hand on top of the partner's hand, he or she can easily regain control over the situation. While your left hand goes to your right shoulder, the right hand can apply a little bit of pressure on the small of your partner's back (*Ming Men* acupressure point). Decisively taking one or two Natural Steps forward will allow you to throw your partner on his or her back. Practice the same method of self-defense with the right hand as well.

Forward Push – Backward Pull

Forward Push – Backward Pull application

Parallel Grip occurs when someone grabs your right hand with his or her left hand and vice versa. If your adventure partner is standing next to you, grabbing your right hand with a Parallel Grip, notice the direction of his or her *Lao Gong* point. If it points forward in relation to your body, step with your right foot back and away from your partner's Centerline and then imitate doing a Forward Push with the right elbow. Just like in the previous combination, you need to fake a Forward Push leaving the grabbing hand in the same spatial position until you switch to doing a Backward Pull. Make sure that your right elbow slides below his or her left elbow. Right away, reverse your movement and make a Backward Pull aiming with the right elbow at his or her *Kua* (the hip crease) and stepping with your right leg directly behind your partner's left leg. This will throw your partner backward on his or her rear end. For your own safety, follow the movement of the falling body to assure that you end up near your partner's head, rather than the feet. Throughout this movement, your left hand needs to be on guard in order to protect your face from any incidental punches. Explore the same combination on the other side.

Closing

Closing uses the second method of bringing the elbow to the Centerline by bringing the hand to the opposite armpit. It is similar in principle to the first method, Forward Push, although it uses a Natural Turn instead of a Natural Step forward. For example, if you perform Closing with the left elbow, begin by lifting the right foot off the ground and turning to the right on the heel of your left foot. Active pivoting of the pelvis in the direction of the Natural Turn initiates the torque of the body that can develop into a centrifugal wave of energy flowing all the way into the elbow.

Closing with the right elbow

As in the previous movements, it is essential to deliver the impact with the elbow strike before the front foot lands, draining the potential energy into the ground. Although you can use this movement to turn 180 degrees or more, it is not important how far you turn when performing Closing; however, it is crucial not to spin yourself out of balance. The back leg stays bent at the knee in such a way that, if you glance down, the knee will be covering the back foot from sight. This will ensure alignment of that foot with the rest of the leg.

The power of Closing combines the qualities of energy projection with Forward Push and Downward Press. The four main principles of energy awareness applicable in Forward Push and Backward Pull are equally relevant in Closing. In addition, lowering of the center of mass is similar to Downward Press. As a result, Closing has a spiraling quality of movement with its vector of force being parallel to the upper arm (*humerus* bone). The more precisely you align your upper arm with this vector, the more you can be sure that the tip of the elbow delivers the strike rather than the "funny bone" located on the side of the elbow.

Opening

As a reversal of Closing, this movement begins from the opposite side of the body as if you are pulling a saber out of its scabbard. Opening may resemble simple dayto-day movements like opening a sliding glass door, or pushing aside heavy curtains. It begins with a sideways Natural Step of the foot on the same side as the opening arm. The movement of the center of mass sideways generates an energy wave flowing all the way into the arm on the same side.

The resulting elbow strike needs to reach the target before the stepping foot lands on the ground. It does not require any turning of the torso in the direction of the target, but rather maintaining a right angle between that direction and your Centerline. You simply need to make a Natural Step sideways; however, you need to turn your head to clearly see your target and to be fully aware whom your elbow is about to strike.

Opening with the left elbow

Symmetry of the torso is very helpful in making your Opening particularly effective. It entails that you maintain alignment of the spine with the median of the angle between your legs. You can explore this alignment when making Natural Steps sideways as your hands slide down your thighs. Test your Symmetry by checking whether both of your hands slide toward the knees at the same pace while you lift one leg and make a step.

Last but not least, after you make a step with one foot, bring the other foot closer in to maintain a comfortable Natural Stance, with your weight evenly distributed between the feet. You can expedite the process of learning Opening by visualizing tracers your elbows leave in the air as if invisible paint brushes are attached to them. Practice Opening with alternating arms while stepping side-to-side and drawing two signs of infinity with your elbows. This will also assist you in developing a smoother and more graceful quality of movement as well as prevent one-sided energy field distortion.

Applications:

Opening – Closing

Opening – Closing application

If your adventure partner grabs your left hand using a Cross Grip with his or her *Lao Gong* point directed to your left, it is a perfect time to use a combination of Opening and Closing. First, imitate Opening with the left arm while positioning your feet away from your partner's Centerline without changing the spatial position of your partner's grabbing hand. Aligning your left forearm with his or her forearm will enable you to turn your palm downwards to get the "upper hand," literally placing your hand on top of your partner's. Then reverse your movement, performing a Closing with the left elbow towards your partner's head or throat. Experiment with simultaneously applying pressure on the small of his or her back using your right hand. Making a decisive motion with your right foot to your right, so that your entire body performs a Natural Turn to the right, should contribute to the effectiveness of this throw. This movement will spin your partner off balance, head towards you and feet away from you. It is preferable for you that your partner lands this way, since he or she will not be able to kick you. Practice the same combination on the other side, too.

Closing – Opening

Closing – Opening application

When your partner grabs your right hand with his or her left hand, *Lao Gong* point of the grabbing hand facing towards your Center, take a Natural Step to the right and make a Natural Turn to the left. Simultaneously, make a Closing with your right arm getting your right elbow above his or her left elbow so that the grabbing hand stays in the same place in space. Make sure your right hip gets next to your partner's left hip. Continue by reversing the direction of your movement and making an Opening with your right elbow aiming at your partner's head or throat. Take one or several Natural Steps to the right during the Opening and continue moving in that direction, behind your partner's back, until he or she collapses backwards over your right leg. Remember to end up standing next to your partner's head so that he or she cannot kick you when falling. During this combination, keep your left hand on guard below your right arm to protect your right side. Also practice this combination when your partner grabs your left hand with a similar Parallel Grip.

Downward Press

Downward Press is the easiest way to project energy downward. This downward wave of energy can flow from the center of your body into your arm and down into your target. Dropping your center of mass will allow you to utilize the force of gravity instead of your physical force. This requires bending the knees, rather than the waist. **"Don't bend over – bend your knees!"** is a popular Qi Dao phrase particularly pertinent in learning Downward Press.

Downward Press with the right elbow

If you make a Downward Press with the right elbow, begin the cascading wave by lifting the left foot simultaneously bending the right leg, which should initiate the movement of your center of mass downwards. The wave-like quality of this motion implies that the movement of the pelvis precedes the movement of the shoulder and the elbow follows the shoulder, not the other way around. The quintessential aspect of Downward Press is timing the impact delivered by the elbow into the target before the opposite foot lands back on the ground. Compare both ways: the elbow striking before the foot lands on the ground versus the elbow striking after the foot has landed. See if you notice how the energy drains into the ground if the foot lands first. This is the same principle that you have learned to apply in all the other basic movements of Qi Dao, except Upper Cut.

To ensure that your elbow is on the Centerline, bring the hand to the same side shoulder, which constitutes the third way to align the elbow with the Centerline. At the same time, the opposite arm can naturally make the reversal movement called Upper Cut. Synchronization of these two movements will prepare the opposite arm for another Downward Press and provide you with head protection in case you use it in martial arts or for self-defense.

The principles of Orientation, Stabilization, Rooting and Streamlining are also relevant in Downward Press. When practicing Downward Press for a while, you may notice that your energy field shifts downwards. To avoid energy deviations, such as pain in your groin and tension in the thighs, do not overdo it or combine it with practicing Upper Cut.

Upper Cut

Upper Cut is a reversal of Downward Press and vice versa. Indeed, where else would the elbow possibly come from to move upward if not from the Downward Press? Yet Upper Cut is arguably the most complex of the basic six directional movements.

You may start learning Upper Cut with the right elbow on your Centerline, right hand near the right shoulder. Visualize a target to your right. Begin your movement by turning your head and then the whole body to face the target, stepping with the right foot directly underneath it. After that, the right elbow begins to move upward and to the side as you pivot inward on the ball of the right foot turning your right side to the target once again. It is crucial to synchronize turning the torso sideways in relation to the target with moving your elbow upward and to the side. In this way, your right elbow keeps pointing at the target all the time. Just before it reaches the target from underneath, straighten the right leg and push the heel into the ground, thrusting the right hip up. This will create a wave flowing through the right side of your body giving the elbow strike adequate power without much exertion of the shoulder muscles. Make sure to keep your sight of the target by turning the head to the right, despite the turning of the torso sideways.

Upper Cut with the left elbow

Upper Cut is the only one of the six directional movements that works best on your opponent's Centerline, since the main target for this movement is the chin, which usually grows on the Centerline. For this and other reasons, the opposite arm needs to perform a secondary movement of Downward Press to balance and protect your body. It is somewhat similar to the placement of the boxer's arm while making a punch with the other arm.

If you practice Upper Cut for a number of repetitions, you may notice some distortion of your energy field that sometimes results in dizziness and/or light-headedness. To avoid these side-effects of shifting your energy field off Center upwards, alternate practicing Upper Cut and Downward Press. Another peculiarity of this movement is the brushing gesture of the open hand towards the back of the head, which occurs when the elbow of that arm is executing Upper Cut. Notice that if your hand goes in front of your face instead, it will likely block your vision or even punch you in the face. Compare and choose which way you like better.

Applications:

Upper Cut – Downward Press

Upper Cut – Downward Press application

When your adventure partner grabs your right hand with his or her right hand facing upward, follow the direction of *Lao Gong* point with a simulated Upper Cut. Your initial motion doesn't even have to be directed towards your partner's head. It can just move in that general direction on the outside of your partner's right elbow. If necessary, help your partner bend his or her right elbow using your other arm's secondary movement. As soon as your elbow reaches the level of his or her head, step with your left foot behind your partner, at the same time, making a Downward Press aiming at his or her throat or collarbone. If you do not want to hurt your practice partner, make this movement slowly and gently; otherwise, follow through by throwing your partner on his or her back. Swift footwork using one or more Natural Steps is essential in completing your maneuver to get behind your partner before he or she realizes what happened.

Keep in mind that this is a very powerful martial art application that can be devastating to the person grabbing you. Therefore, be mindful when working with your partner, because he or she will also be practicing on you (*Karma* has a tendency to come back many fold). Do not forget to practice the same combination with your left arm.

Downward Press – Upper Cut

Downward Press – Upper Cut application

Your adventure partner's best bet in controlling you is by holding your hand on his or her Centerline, *Lao Gong* point pointing downwards. If he or she grabs your left hand, make a feint Downward Press with your left elbow while protecting your head with your right arm using a secondary movement of Upper Cut. Align your left forearm with your partner's forearm without moving his or her grabbing hand. As soon as you elicit your partner's reaction in the form of resistance to your feigning the Downward Press, turn your left palm up and step with your left foot between his or her feet. Immediately proceed with an accurate Upper Cut targeting your partner's chin with your left elbow, but be careful not to break his or her jaw (do not forget about *Karma*). As long as you're not rushing your partner to the emergency room, continue by experimenting with this combination on the opposite side.

Moving with the Energy Ball

With practice, you may find that the six directional movements presented in this chapter can be practiced with the hands holding an imaginary ball of energy. This will allow you to learn how to make your movements particularly smooth, fluid, and harmonious. Both hands can naturally perform primary and secondary movements in synch with each other when holding the energy ball from two opposite sides. For example, when making a Forward Push with the left elbow, bring the left hand to the right shoulder as if it is resting on the energy ball that you support with the right hand from underneath. The right hand simultaneously makes a secondary movement of Backward Pull until you switch the hands around the energy ball, alternating the actions of your hands. As the hands slide around the surface of this *Qi* ball, the right hand now reaches the left shoulder making a secondary Forward Push with the right elbow while the left hand supports the energy ball from below performing a primary Backward Pull.

There are several ways to practice these movements. You can start by using one and the same elbow to perform the primary movements of Forward Push and Backward Pull while the opposite elbow is making only secondary movements. You can combine these movements with steps back and forth, making a tap with the foot before it makes a step. Tapping the ground as if bouncing with the ball of the foot off the floor helps generate greater waves flowing all the way to your elbows. The moment of tapping the ground with the foot would ideally coincide with the moment of switching the hands around your ball of energy.

Such timing would also allow you to make sure that the primary movement delivers the impact into the target a split-second before the stepping foot lands on the ground. The tap will delay that foot in the air for a spilt second, which is all you will need to reach the target with the elbow first. Without this delay, the energy of your Natural Step would drain through your foot into the ground instead of impacting the target, which is what would make you resort to using force instead of power.

Alternatively, you can switch from one arm to the other in performing primary movements. For example, moving forward with steps along a zigzag line, as if you are skating, allows you to practice Forward Push as a primary movement with alternating arms. The tap before each step becomes even more necessary in this case, because it enables you to synchronize your steps with the movements of the arms. Another example is going backwards with alternating Backward Pulls. The secondary movement of Forward Push should not be neglected here either, because, among other reasons, it is supposed to empower your primary movement.

Opening and Closing can also be practiced using the image of the *Qi* ball to facilitate the non-stop movement of the arms following a trajectory resembling the sign of infinity. Start with making Openings as primary movements on both sides alternating your Natural Steps from one side to the other. Coordinate the movements of your arms so that the energy ball comes up on the Centerline and goes down on your side and then comes back to the Centerline again and goes down on the other side. The arm making a secondary Closing movement continuously follows the other arm until the hands switch around the energy ball and trade roles. This moment of switching would ideally coincide with the tap of the foot that is ready to make another step sideways.

You may explore making primary movements of Opening and Closing with the same arm. Please notice that Closing is always done with a Natural Turn while the Opening requires a simple Natural Step sideways without any turning of the torso. This means you will gradually be turning around while practicing these movements. Make sure you switch to the opposite side and perform the same movements while gradually turning in the opposite direction to prevent getting dizzy. To complete this practice, explore Closing as your primary movement with alternating arms while turning around 180 degrees and doing Opening as a secondary movement. You may notice that tapping the floor with the rear foot makes it much easier to perform a Natural Turn and observe the same kind of timing as in Forward Push.

You can practice Downward Press and Upper Cut in a similar fashion, too. Imagine the energy ball in a shape of a round helmet on your head that you can twist around. Each hand can slide around the head from the back of the neck to the same-side shoulder and back. When you perform Downward Press with the right arm, your right hand moves to the right shoulder while your left hand slides behind the back of the neck as you make an Upper Cut with the left elbow; and vise versa. Once again, you may begin by practicing Downward Press as your primary movement with alternating arms. Do not forget to tap before making each step with the foot opposite the elbow performing Downward Press, which will help you lift your center of mass before descending down.

When you switch to practicing Upper Cut as your primary movement, imagine your targets positioned directly to your right and to your left so that you make 180-degree turns with each step. To make your energy field balanced, I suggest you alternate practicing Upper Cut and Downward Press as primary movements with the same arm while doing the secondary movements with the other arm. This will test your coordination and sense of alignment, because you will be turning almost 180 degrees from the higher target for the Upper Cut to the lower target on the other side for the Downward Press.

I hope you remember the Chinese phrase *"Qi Dao Yi Dao."* With practice, this ball of energy will become your magical ally providing you with guidance and power. Developing a reasonable degree of proficiency in the Harmonious Culture of Movement usually takes three to six months, depending on how much you practice and how quickly you learn. If you combine mastering these practices with receiving Qi Dao Coaching from me or another certified Qi Dao coach, you will be able to receive initiation into the practice of Empowerment. This would also make you a member of our Shamanic tribe of spiritual adventurers, who enjoy various opportunities to travel and practice together promoting each other's levels of mastery and awareness. For more information about the Qi Dao initiation, visit www.qidao.org/initiation.

The practice of Empowerment, which forms the foundation for more advanced Qi Dao practices, can be described as meditation on the movements that spontaneously follow the flow of the energy ball. Instead of moving the energy ball as you please, you will learn to let this field of energy move you in the most spontaneous and unpredictable ways. As I mentioned in the introduction to this book, dream being can be considered both a noun and a verb. The practice of Empowerment is like being in a lucid dream, knowing that everything manifests the way it should and enjoying the ride.

If you want to become an embodiment of being in the flow, you may need to fine-tune your energy awareness. You will find it fairly easy to start perceiving *Qi* while enjoying the first guided meditation called Lucid Daydreaming from the meditation CD entitled Qi Dao Initiation (which can be ordered online at www.qidao.org/cd101) guiding you to imagine experiencing whatever you can dream of. You can just engage your imagination and experiment with the basic Qi Dao movements while visualizing an energy ball between your hands. You can also boost your energy sensitivity by using a so-called Tai Chi Ruler or a short stick about one foot long. Move around holding its opposing ends between the centers of your palms, so that your hands are constantly a foot apart. It will be challenging to practice Upper Cut and Downward Press with the Tai Chi Ruler, because it will need to be moving side to side behind your head. For that reason, you may use a belt wrapped around your hands to keep them about one foot apart. After a few weeks or months of this practice, you may find you no longer need any device to aid you in feeling the ball of energy between your hands and sensing the flow of *Qi*.

Chapter Five: Element of Earth Kicks

Kicking is another way to project energy – this time using your legs instead your arms. Just as you started exploring energy projection with your arms using your elbows before learning how to use hands (which is the subject of the intermediate level of Qi Dao studies), I suggest that you start with your knees before using feet. The reason for this progression is very simple: it is much easier to send a wave into the knee than into the foot due to the distance from the energy Center of the body. Since it is generally easier to project energy waves from the center on shorter distances, it would be even easier to send the waves into your hips… if you could only bring your hips into alignment with your Centerline.

Similar to most of the elbow strikes that do not have to start from a Natural Stance, knee kicks are usually done with the rear leg, given that the other one is your front leg. Whenever kicking requires an extra step prior to launching the knee, feel free to experiment with the distance you need to cover with that step. Obviously, working on a target (such as your padded sticks) held by your adventure partner should contribute to developing precision and fluidity of your movements. When you practice following up with an elbow strike, ask your partner to hold two sticks at higher and lower levels.

As you produce kicks with the knees, engage your arms in holding the energy ball and making adequate follow-through movements. Each one of these movements can be compared to getting in touch with the head of your opponent just a second before the kick. If you have a really adventuresome practice partner, you may slowly practice your kicks on him or her in this manner. Make sure to reciprocate by letting him or her use you as a target, too. With practice, you will learn to appreciate being on the receiving end of energy projections. This practice will require being in the flow, attentive, natural and awake. **Practicing the Foundational Principles of Qi Dao under pressure is indispensable if you want to physically embody them.**

Lotus Kick

Lotus Kick may be considered a combination of the rotation of your leg bent at the knee from inside outwards with Natural Turn. The leg rotation, which we have already explored in the context of Harmonious Culture of Movement, may be done with quite a bit of momentum. The more momentum your leg has, the higher your foot will swing at the climax of the movement. This rotation by itself does not require any pivoting, but when combined with the pivoting on the heel of the standing foot, it produces a powerful kick projecting energy spiraling upward and around you.

Lotus Kick with the left knee

For the sake of safety of your joints consider the most advantageous angle of the knee meeting the target. Compare hitting a soft target with the lateral side of your knee versus the kneecap. You may discover a noticeable difference between these two methods of kicking. The former exposes your knee to the dangerous impact from the side while the latter keeps your leg in alignment. Leg alignment is as crucial in kicking as it is in standing or stepping. As an exaggerated Natural Turn, this kick works in concord with all the principles of Harmonious Culture of Movement you have learned by now.

Ability to follow through with other movements following the kick is a vital aspect of all Qi Dao kicks. Many beginning students have a tendency to fall through instead of following through after their kicks. If your foot lands too heavily after the kick, you may notice you have to expend more energy in order to continue your movements with balance and gracefulness. This issue can be ameliorated quite easily by bouncing off the ground with the landing foot as soon as you complete your kick, which means taking an extra step right after kicking. Imagine that your foot can bounce off the floor like a basketball when you dribble it. You may even practice dribbling your leg with the same side hand, quickly pushing it down and letting it bounce back up. When your foot lands completing the extra step, make sure to observe all the pertinent alignments (i.e., Orientation, Stabilization, Grounding, Rooting, etc). This extra step will allow you to regain total balance and enable you to follow through with appropriate movements after your Lotus Kick as well as any other type of kicks.

I would like to invite you to experiment with each of the six directional arm movements in order to find your favorite one to follow-up your Lotus Kick with. Compare and choose the combination that you resonate with; however, do not expect to find the ultimate solution right away. Try every movement at least a couple of times in combination with this kick to sense how its energy flows with the energy of the kick. I am sure that you will have much fun with various awkward combinations before finding the one that works (a hint: match the direction of the energy flow of the kick).

Roundhouse Kick

Roundhouse Kick may be considered a combination of the rotation of your leg bent at the knee from outside inwards with the pivoting on the ball of the standing foot in the direction of the kick. Unlike Lotus Kick, Roundhouse goes beyond the principle of Natural Turn in terms of kicking with the leg opposite the direction of turning. Please note that there is a great difference between turning inwards versus outwards. Turn inwards on the ball of the foot and then on the heel for the sake of comparison. You may find it rather awkward (if possible at all) to turn inwards on your heel, unlike turning outwards, which is much easier done on the heel than the ball of the foot. Compare and make your own choice as to your favorite way to turn in either direction.

The Symmetry principle certainly applies to this kick. It means that you can use your upper body to counter balance the kicking leg with the spine following the median of the angle between the thighs. Observe the alignment of your neck to check whether it follows the tilt of the rest of the spine.

Roundhouse Kick with the right knee

Just like Lotus Kick, Roundhouse also requires awareness of the part of the knee that hits the target. I could invite you to try hitting the target in various ways again but I have more compassion than that. To spare you from unnecessary pain and suffering, I simply suggest turning your kneecap toward the target to save the medial side of the knee from bruising or injury. In order to achieve this, your lower leg needs to reach the height of the knee at the moment of impact. An easy practice that can improve your flexibility in this direction consists of lifting your leg completely bent at the knee and grasping the foot with the same side hand while using the opposite hand to guide the knee to horizontal alignment. This precarious position may challenge your balance, which makes it a nice balancing exercise as well.

As a result of this knee alignment, your landing foot should be pigeon-toed at the moment of landing. At the same time, your Centerline is going to turn ninety or more degrees away from your target challenging your balance and Orientation. You can re-orient and re-stabilize yourself by bouncing with the ball of that foot off the ground to make an extra step. You may opt for small Natural Turns instead of steps if you spin past your target. This extra turn also serves as an indicator of following through or falling through after the kick, because it is virtually impossible to perform a decent Natural Turn when falling through. On the other hand, following through with another kick or elbow strike is easy when you take this extra turn and regain Stabilization by aligning both your landing foot and Centerline with the target while shifting more than fifty percent of your weight on that foot.

Test every one of the six directional arm movements in order to find the one suitable for follow-up after Roundhouse. Experiment with each elbow strike, in combination with this kick, at least a few times, to sense how its energy can initiate another kick. Remember which one of the six directional movements requires a Natural Turn? Making that particular elbow strike after your Roundhouse will enable you to make another Roundhouse with the opposite knee right away. Find out for yourself which combination works best for you.

Front Kick

Front Kick is usually performed with the knee of the rear leg. If you just lift the rear foot off the ground, you will start falling backwards as with Natural Step backward. In order to create forward momentum, take a Natural Step forward with your front foot. As soon as all your weight shifts on the front foot, the back foot will be ready to leave the ground to launch a Front Kick. Lifting the knee on your Centerline will give it maximum power, in case you run into your target sooner than expected. Continue the movement with your knee pointing directly towards your target while pivoting on the ball of the standing foot in the fashion similar to Roundhouse. You may compare the strength of your kick with and without such a turn. You may also test turning on the ball versus the heel of the standing foot. To make the difference in power and stability even more dramatic, try bringing the heel of the standing foot back on the ground at the moment of delivering the impact. Compare the results and choose the method of turning which resonates with you best.

Front Kick with the right knee

Just as in other knee kicks, Front Kick needs to reach the target with the tip of the kneecap to produce maximum effect. The kicking knee will be away from your Centerline by the time you complete this movement. Explore whether you can enhance your stability by tracking the toes of the standing foot with your Centerline while pivoting, so that by the end of the kick your navel will end up facing about ninety degrees away from the target. Your upper body can counter-balance the kicking leg by tilting slightly back and then sideways (in alignment with the median of the angle between your thighs) as you proceed with the kick.

As soon as your foot returns to the ground, you can return to facing the target again by bouncing off the ground with the ball of that foot and taking a small step forward, shifting more than fifty percent of your weight on the front foot. Notice that this extra step can be used as a Natural Step preceding Front Kick with the other leg. This allows you to follow through with another kick right away. You can test this idea by making a series of Front Kicks with intermittent extra steps. It may also be used as a step to produce an elbow strike with the opposite elbow. Take your time to find out which one of the six arm movements would be the best follow-up after Front Kick. Hopefully, you will find it fairly easy to combine that particular kind of elbow strike and Front Kick in a series of alternating arm and leg movements. The kick should follow the elbow strike on the same side: right elbow strike – right Front Kick – left elbow strike – left Front Kick, and so on. **I challenge you to find a better way to learn sending powerful waves through your entire body than practicing this combination of movements.** Make sure to observe all body alignments while moving in this manner. To allow more room for experimentation, add the imagery of the *Qi* ball.

Self-defense Applications

The three knee kicks introduced in this chapter may become indispensable tools for defending yourself if someone tries to kick you. Qi Dao does not teach any blocks, because blocks attempt to stop the flow of your opponent's energy. Going against the flow of the energy of an attack is the epitome of reacting instead of responding to the challenge. By the way, using your arms against kicks is often less than optimal, since your opponent's legs are likely to be stronger and longer than your arms. As soon as you develop enough gracefulness and precision with your kicks, you will be able to use them to prevent or divert any oncoming knee kick.

Lotus Kick defense against a Front Kick with a knee

To kick off your self-defense practice, ask your adventure partner to kick you slowly in the stomach using Front Kick with the left leg. As soon as you notice the kick approaching your body, launch Lotus Kick with your left leg to intercept and divert his or her kick just slightly past your body. Ideally, you will end up behind your partner's back, where you will be able to do whatever you have to do in order to prevent any further attacks. Make sure you do not hurt your practice partner though, for your kick may be hitting a weak area on the side of his or her knee. Experiment with the same method of self-defense on the other side.

Roundhouse Kick defense against a Roundhouse Kick with a knee

When your adventure partner attempts to attack you using Roundhouse Kick with the left leg, you can also use Roundhouse with your right leg. There are two options for this response: you may merge the oncoming kick with your left knee getting either under the partner's knee or above it. In both cases, you just need to continue the momentum of the oncoming kick and turn your partner around, so that you again end up behind his or her back. If your partner is adventurous enough to attempt continuing his or her spin in order to face you again, follow through with a pacifying elbow strike. In our future books we will explore recycling as a method of returning *Qi* back into the person's energy system. It is very healing although not always pleasant, depending on that person's choice whether to relax standing or to relax on the ground. Make sure to practice Roundhouse defense on the opposite side as well.

If your partner makes a Lotus Kick with his or her left leg, you can thwart the attack by making a Front Kick with your left leg. Once again, you should end up behind his or her back, which is a very advantageous position. Your adventure partner may try to continue the attack by attempting Upper Cut with the right elbow. All you need to do about this threat is to challenge his or her balance by following through with an extra step after your Front Kick. Do not forget to explore the same application on the right side, too.

Front Kick defense against a Lotus Kick with a knee

These are a few simple examples of going with the flow of *Qi* projected at you rather than opposing it. Qi Dao requires going beyond intellectual understanding of this principle by exercising it regularly. If you embody this principle utilizing Harmonious Culture of Movement, you will become an embodiment of your knowledge, capable of translating it into all other spheres of your life. Ultimately, Qi Dao teaches you to **transcend any opposition and turn your opponents into friends by assisting them in uncovering and manifesting their own deepest, most profound dreams.**

Chapter Six: Holding Patterns

One of the benefits of becoming familiar with our Harmonious Culture of Movement is that it should encourage you to pay attention to your habitual ways of holding tension in various muscles in your body. Most people have a tendency to constantly maintain a certain degree of tension as though they are going to fall apart if they stop holding themselves together. Additionally, chronic tension in any particular area of the body cannot exist without counter-balancing tensions in many other parts of the body, which results in a whole-body pattern of holding tension. As a result of habituation, up to eighty or even ninety percent of human energy potential may be spent on maintaining personal holding patterns.

As numerous experiments undeniably demonstrate, tension impedes the flow of *Qi* and creates energetic blockages that lead to energy deficiency in the affected areas of the body. The disempowered parts of the body include not only the weakened muscles and restricted joints; blood and lymph circulation are also restricted by chronic tension, which affects many internal organs and systems of the body. Any holding pattern can create chronic pain and discomfort, limiting range of motion and restricting energy flow throughout the organism.

As we discovered earlier, tension is a process that requires doing, sending signals through the nervous system to tell the muscles to contract. It cannot be undone by doing more, because relaxation requires you to stop sending these signals rather than doing anything extra. Letting go of tension requires being attentive to the tense area of the body. This will help you realize that you have been doing something and choose whether to keep doing it from now on. Do you remember the adage, "energy flows wherever awareness goes?" Being attentive to any tense and hence weak muscles will empower them to become stronger and more relaxed.

The way you experience yourself by and large depends on your awareness. You may often be aware of pain in a tense muscle but not your habitual imbalance throughout the body. Generally speaking, you are less likely to notice your habitual pattern than some immediate changes in that pattern.

If you find yourself wishing you could get rid of your tension, then you need to accept and learn the lessons presented by your holding patterns in order to integrate your new awareness into a more harmonious way of being. If you agree that everything that ever happened to you was supposed to happen, given your energy that was supportive of the way things unfolded in your life, then you may also consider that your holding pattern is exactly what you needed to experience in your body up until now. You can appreciate it as a catalyst for personal transformation providing you with a great lesson about experiencing life as you dream it up. As my friend, Lama Surya Das puts it, "**let go of the person you used to be**," so that you can be who you dream of being. In other words, the grand dream of Dream Being can be revealed and manifested by living your dreams.

From a very young age, your bodily movements naturally played an essential role in your emotional life as *somatic* (physical) expressions of your feelings and emotions. Conversely, if expressing your emotions was uncomfortable or unacceptable as you were growing up, you might feel like you needed to suppress your feelings by inhibiting your expressiveness. You might choose to restrain your movements by developing tension if you felt inadequate or scared to express your feelings freely. As you were growing up and developing your unique personality, you were also developing your particular way of holding yourself. This inhibition through tension might have appeared necessary for your emotional well-being, since it allowed you to prevent exposing your feelings through spontaneous movements. Any holding pattern can be perceived as a survival tool that can help you go through some challenging experiences without feeling as if you are falling apart.

There is a strong correlation between certain emotional states and movements of the body through which they can be expressed. Your holding patterns represent the sum total of unmanifest movements that could potentially express the feelings associated with your habitual states of consciousness. Each pattern of tension is essentially a frozen movement as if you stopped in the midst of moving forward, downward, inward, backward, outward or upward. You could say that, **any chronic tension is unmanifest, or frozen, movement**, which morphs your energy field according to the way of being you identify with. This forces the location of the Center of your energy field from being Centered, free to move in any direction, to some other, contrived position. Naturally, any deviation of your energy Center from the center of mass of your body results in a struggle against the imbalance, which requires physical tension.

The most basic patterns of holding tension correspond to the six directional movements described above. While there are many possible ways to hold tension, the following six patterns seem to be the most typical: Holding Forth, Holding Down, Holding In, Holding Back, Holding Out and Holding Up. Most people do not fall under just one category but have two or even three patterns mixed together. These simplified categories serve as tools for greater understanding of human *psyche*, for these holding patterns are physical and energetic representations of human archetypes.

These archetypal states of consciousness dream up corresponding realms of existence complete with their specific ways of perception, attitudes, relationships, health and other issues. Therefore, the way you experience your life now depends more on your current beliefs and identity (energy resonance with a certain way of being) rather than your upbringing or other circumstances. Change your way of thinking and your consciousness will function on a different energy frequency, consequently manifesting a different realm of being.

This is not unlike switching from one radio channel to another by tuning into different frequencies of radio waves. When tuned into a frequency that carries signals transmitted by a radio station, your imaginary receiver will begin to talk or play some music. In a similar fashion, your energy field is like a receiver capable of tuning into different programs broadcast by Dream Being all at once. None of these channels is better or worse than any other one, just as pain from one holding pattern is no better or worse than pain from any other. They allow you to experience the limitations of being stuck in just one realm, perhaps, so that you become more motivated to integrate all the pieces of the puzzle into the whole picture of the dream called your life.

The ability to identify and appreciate your own patterns can help you discover dreams hidden beneath the tensions and pains in your body. To manifest those dreams, you ought to integrate different emotions frozen in your body and transcend any stereotypical ways of thinking or rigid belief systems. This will also require exploring and expanding your psychological comfort zone, because, **similar to your deepest dreams and aspirations, most of your potential can be found outside of your comfort zone**. Had it been otherwise, you would have surely actualized your potential by now.

An unrestricted flow of energy will promote natural healing and integration of your body-mind and spirit. Integrating formerly disconnected parts of you is like helping them manifest their own dreams of health and happiness. Let me reiterate a Qi Dao truism once again, **"The more you help all the different parts of your being manifest their dreams, the more they will help you manifest yours."**

Holding Forth

There is an English expression, "to hold forth," which means talking or moving a lot, and this holding pattern enables you to do exactly that. If you protrude your head forward, your voice will project more, as your whole energy field shifts off your center forward. When Holding Forth, you can usually push forward quite easily but may have difficulty pulling backward. Your physical body is constantly trying to keep from falling forward, hence the muscular tension specific to Holding Forth.

You may see many examples of this pattern in people around you, often in combination with other patterns of holding tension. Even sitting, many people have a tendency to keep Holding Forth. It is particularly noticeable in those drivers who hold their heads forward as if someone is pulling them in that direction by the nose. This holding pattern may be responsible for road rage and other belligerent behaviors on the road.

Holding Forth pattern of tension

On one hand, Holding Forth is a *somatic* manifestation of a self-serving, egocentric and competitive "type A" personality. If you find yourself creating conflicts with others, that may be an expression of your unconscious belief that your survival and/or success are more important than everyone else's. Even if aggressiveness served you well as a survival mechanism in the past, I invite you to question its effectiveness and compare with other ways of relating to others. It may perpetuate a vicious cycle of conflicts, with your presence and demeanor unconsciously projecting this aggressive energy. Indeed, it may be hard to achieve conflict resolution with body language delivering a conflicting message.

On the other hand, Holding Forth can be viewed as a necessary skill when it comes to asserting your position or projecting influence. Your voice becomes heard and your energy appears unstoppable. Consciously choosing when to apply one holding pattern or another will ensure fluid and skillful use of your energy in any situation. What is essential to learn first and foremost though is how to be Centered, which is an embodiment of equanimity.

Realm of Consciousness

To discover or to reconnect with this pattern of holding tension, imagine yourself turning into a wild animal, a beast that can be assertive, self-serving, pushy or even aggressive when necessary. Think for a moment, "Things are going to be my way or the highway!" Even without trying to hold yourself in any specific way, you will, most likely, find yourself Holding Forth. There is really nothing wrong with this way of being as long as it is serves as an appropriate response to the demands of your life. When it is not necessary, however, Holding Forth can waste a lot of your energy and cause undue tension and pain in many areas of the body.

Postural Characteristics

As you work on developing your awareness of tension in the muscle groups involved in this holding pattern, you may first notice that it makes your head protrude forward. This is one of the signatures of this pattern, which requires tension in the back of the neck, since the bones of the neck no longer support the weight of the head. Play with this tension by slowly increasing and decreasing it, so that you develop an acute sense of connection with this muscle group. By learning to contract and relax these muscles at will, you will eventually learn to let go of that tension whenever it is not needed.

While Holding Forth, notice tension in the muscles of the upper back called *rhomboids* and *trapezius* that originate from pulling the shoulders back. The shoulders usually have to be pulled backward in order to compensate for the shift of the head forward; however, there may be variations of this tension resulting from combining this pattern of holding tension with others. Experiment with this tension to find out for yourself whether you have to have it when Holding Forth. In addition to your head, your whole torso may be tilting forward producing more or less chronic tension in *erector spinae* muscles, which form the longest muscle group in human body running the entire length of your spine from the *skull* to the *sacrum*.

Since the morphing of your energy field associated with this holding pattern shifts the center of mass forward, you may notice a characteristic tension in the calves due to distributing more weight on the toes and balls of the feet. If you spend some time paying attention to the way your feet connect to the ground, you will discover the difference between the ways your feet feel when you are Neutral versus Holding Forth. Your knowledge of the principle of Grounding should assist you in this discovery.

Exploring Holding Forth

Practicing Forward Push is one way to explore this holding pattern. Paradoxically, it is what Qi Dao recommends in order to develop full appreciation of Holding Forth, since the direction of the shift in your energy field in this case is also forward. Exaggerating this pattern with Forward Push may expose some neglected or suppressed aspects of your consciousness that may seek your attention by causing discomfort or pain. **Becoming conscious of your unconscious processes can enable you to integrate even those aspects of your being that you would initially want to suppress or get rid of**.

To recognize how counterproductive it is to attempt forcing yourself against your existing energy flow, feel free to experiment with trying to shift your energy field backwards using Backward Pull. After a little while, having encountered the edges of your comfort zone in both directions, you may choose to explore some other possibilities of directional movement: Opening, Closing, Upper Cut and Downward Press. If you find that your energy resonates with a certain direction of movement, you might as well enjoy moving in that direction. Consider that by doing so you can eventually find yourself at the center of your energy field, which should feel quite different from trying to pull the energy field to align it with your physical body. Most likely, you will find it very rewarding to expand your energy field so that it eventually becomes more Neutral and Centered.

Holding Back

If you ever experienced the feeling that something is "holding you back," restricting your ability to accomplish your goals or manifest your dreams, consider a possibility that it might be you holding yourself back. Holding Back pattern has a lot to do with being judgmental about something or someone, or even disgusted with them. Since we all have a tendency to project our feelings and attitudes onto others, we begin to think that others exhibit some unpleasant or downright horrible qualities of character. As you may have realized by now, **you are likely to judge**

those qualities in others that you currently do not identify with. If you have not learned this lesson, Holding Back will serve you as a reminder to pay more attention to your own "buttons." I do not want to say that tension will persist until you improve your character, but rather until you embrace your weaknesses and integrate every aspect of your being – the Dream Being that you are.

Holding Back pattern of tension

To quote a colleague of mine, Sakyong Mipham Rinpoche, "**the confidence of contentment arises from being friendly to ourselves and merciful to others**." As I mentioned in the beginning of this book, acceptance and contentment are the prerequisites for learning whatever you are here to learn about yourself and life in general.

Qi Dao does not promote perceiving anything in black and white fashion; therefore acceptance and rejection are merely shades of gray, as it were. None of the character traits manifesting as holding patterns are simply good or bad. Light and darkness are merely degrees of brightness of the light of consciousness that you shed on certain aspects of your personality and its *somatic* manifestation, your body. Similarly, enlightenment comes and goes in waves as you awaken to certain truths about the nature of existence and fall asleep just to awaken again sooner or later. The more you get used to shining the light of consciousness on your idiosyncrasies, the more enlightened they become – full of energy and no longer weak spots or buttons that can be pushed – thereby facilitating your enlightenment.

Realm of Consciousness

The realm of consciousness associated with this Holding Pattern can easily be experienced if you just assume a dissatisfied, disillusioned or judgmental point of view. Imagine yourself saying with an appropriate facial expression, "Why does everything have to be so annoying?" Uttering this phrase may remind you of someone you know personally; if so, visualize that person and notice his or her holding pattern. That is right, even in your visions and dreams, people usually exhibit certain patterns of tension, movement, speech, and other expressions revealing their energies. Now, do you believe that your dream characters have their own energies or do they rather reflect back to you certain aspects of your energy? How enlightened are you, for instance, if you think that you live in a stupid world full of stupid people? As a fellow Bön lama Tenzin Wangyal Rinpoche explains, "When we look from a dualistic viewpoint, we see an imperfect world and we live as troubled, imperfect beings in that imperfect world. **When we see the world in its perfection, just as it is, we are Buddhas, living in a pure land, surrounded by other Buddhas.**" (In Bön, unlike in Buddhism, we often use the Sanskrit term Buddha in reference to any spiritually awake person.)

Postural Characteristics

To experience the peculiar postural characteristics of Holding Back pattern, imagine that someone is offering you a bowl full of worms to eat! You will probably express your disgust by pulling away from such a repulsive treat. When Holding Back, you can experience tension in a specific combination of muscle groups: *SCM* (muscles on the front of the neck) due to the head being pulled back; *pectoralis major* (chest muscles) from pulling the shoulders forward to counterbalance the head; *abs, gluteus* and *hamstrings* tilting the pelvis backward; and *tibialis anterior* (shin muscles) that keep you from falling backwards as you balance on the heels. Your weight naturally shifts towards your heels when your entire energy field morphs backwards. Hold yourself in this position for a while to recognize the challenges it presents to a person Holding Back all the time. Notice how much easier it is to walk backward than forward when Holding Back. No wonder people holding themselves in this manner tend to feel as if they are being held back from reaching their goals!

Exploring Holding Back

To test the flow of energy specific to this holding pattern, play a game of tug of war with your partner. Together, grab one of your sticks and apply Backward Pull to compare your strength while Holding Back versus holding yourself in any other manner. Notice whether your partner's holding pattern makes any difference in his or her strength when pulling back. Just to humor me, try Forward Push while Holding Back. This experiment should make it abundantly clear why you cannot advance while Holding Back and maintaining a judgmental attitude.

Practicing Backward Pull can help you discover the true nature of this holding pattern. Even if you find yourself Holding Back in your daily life, you can learn to perceive it as a lesson rather than a problem that needs to be fixed. If this is the case, Qi Dao would suggest exaggerating your Holding Back pattern by practicing Backward Pull, which might bring to the surface some aspects of your consciousness that have been unconsciously holding you back. Indeed, **Holding Back pattern is a *somatic* manifestation of the inner critic**.

In addition to exploring your comfort zone by trying to push your energy field forward, experiment with other possible directions of movement: Opening, Closing, Upper Cut and Downward Press. Once again, feel the energy resonance and allow it to guide you in the direction that will restore your balance. With practice, you will find a new alignment with your energy field and transcend whatever holding patterns you have.

Holding In

You can usually notice that a person is Holding In by the restrictions in his or her movements, breathing and general physical capabilities. Holding In makes one's speech short and timid, as well as other expressions revealing one's psychological tension. Being physically tense is usually a *somatic* manifestation of emotional tension. One has to be in a particular state of mind to achieve such a high level of tension – the state of fear.

Whether one's fear is expressed or suppressed, it shrinks one's energy field and shuts down *Qi* circulation. The energy field of the person in fear is shrinking from the world that appears to be a scary place. The attitude representing this holding pattern is one of cautiousness and lack of trust, being afraid of opening up to life.

Holding In pattern of tension

While love is a process of expanding your energy field, fear is a process of diminishing or shrinking it. If you hold onto your feeling of fear long enough, it can become your habitual *modus operandi* (mode of operation or *MO* for short). Qi Dao does not preach to eliminate fear forever and be all love; it rather recognizes fear as one of the natural human emotions. Taking into consideration that people have a tendency to create rigid identities out of their habitual states, Qi Dao teaches to transcend attachment to the old sense of self expressed through holding patterns. It is not really your holding patterns that you are working on – it is your sense of identity attached to the states of consciousness manifesting as your patterns of holding tension that you are learning to surrender.

You can easily let go of any undue fears and anxieties by learning to be present. Right now, while reading these words, check whether you have anything to be scared of at the present moment. You can find that most fears are not about the present moment but about the future, which is a dream woven out of the memories of the past. Now you have a choice whether to be reactive and scared of things that you dream up or to be responsive and creative in your daydream. Whatever *MO* you identify with at the moment, you tune into the corresponding scenario that manifests out of the countless probabilities available to you all the time. **Your whole life manifests moment by moment as your energy aligns with the flow of the life situations that it resonates with**.

Realm of Consciousness

To experience the Holding In pattern of tension, imagine being a frightened dog, tucking its tail between its legs and trying to seem smaller. You can also use the image of a tortoise hiding its head and limbs in its shell to protect itself from danger. "What allows me to survive is caution, rather than trust." Notice the pattern in which muscles throughout your body respond to such mental images. As with other holding patterns, Holding In can serve as a survival mechanism that is usable in danger or under emotional pressure. Perhaps, you too might have used it as a child or adolescent to make yourself a smaller target (literally or metaphorically). Of course, this is just one of many ways to deal with challenging situations in life. **The practice of Qi Dao teaches you to relax under pressure, which is a superb method for dealing with stress that will make you an embodiment of being in the flow**.

Postural Characteristics

There are several specific areas in the body that will likely have the most tension when Holding In: shoulders, groin and inner thighs. Tension in the muscles of the neck called *scalenes* along with *trapezius* results from pulling the head into the shoulders. It is the most pronounced hallmark of this holding pattern, for virtually everyone tends to suck the head into its trunk like a scared or shocked turtle. Most people in distress also tend to clench their fists, which can be contributed to the grasping reflex particularly noticeable in small children. Such a hypertension, also known as high blood pressure, is one of the main health hazards associated with stress, which is a result of "fight or flight" reaction to living in fear.

You may also experience tension in *peroneus* – the muscles on the lateral sides of the lower legs due to shifting more weight on the inner edges of the feet. You may notice *inversion* of your knees due to the excessive tension in *adductors* and *pectineus* (the muscles of the inner thighs and groin). This misalignment of the legs can make you rather unstable. Test it by asking your partner to push you from any direction. Your partner should be able to push you over effortlessly when you are Holding In.

Exploring Holding In

Closing is the movement projecting energy inward and is particularly easy to perform while Holding In. Opening, on the other hand, may pose quite a challenge, since it requires openness to the outward flow of energy, which is not easy when you are Holding In. To learn the lessons presented by this Holding Pattern, Qi Dao would suggest exploring the edge of the comfort zone by playing with Opening and Closing, which may make shrinking of your energy field even more apparent. This is supposed to bring you face-to-face with some of your deepest fears, quintessentially, with the fear of death. **Facing your fear is usually the most direct way to see through it and to transcend it**.

Imagine that there is a movie created about your entire life similar to the flashback reported by those who survived near-death experiences. As with most movies, the last episode in your film can potentially reveal the meaning and purpose of the whole picture. However uncomfortable it may feel thinking about dying, consider that today is a good day to die, since you never know when you may expire and quit dreaming this particular dream. Today, you can accept your mortality and live your most fearless day on earth consciously manifesting your life's purpose. Obviously, if you do not happen to die today, you will have an opportunity to live another day being even more aware of the meaning of life than before. This is a simple but profound way to transform your life into a chain of powerful steps, each one more momentous than the one before.

Carlos Castaneda's Don Juan would say that "…**happiness is to act with the full knowledge that [you] don't have time**." I wholeheartedly agree that using death as your personal advisor can fill your acts with amazing power and bless your life with love and freedom.

Holding Out

When you are Holding Out for something, it means that you feel skeptical or unconvinced about whatever has been offered to you and are waiting to find something more interesting or exciting. You may observe that people standing in line at a store often have a tendency to strike a very particular pose. It is similar to the military "at ease" stance with more weight on one leg. Many people believe that shifting weight on one leg allows them to be more relaxed; however, it actually requires quite a bit of muscular tension throughout the body.

When I was much younger, I used to wonder why so many of my students exhibited this peculiar Holding Pattern until I realized that I was also Holding Out to some extent. As it were, I was dreaming up others to demonstrate the very idiosyncrasy I could not notice in myself. As I accepted and learned whatever I could from this Holding Pattern, most of my students radically transformed and quit Holding Out. Some of them eventually mentioned to me that I was their role model of body awareness and as soon as I changed, they followed suit. I responded by asking them to ponder on the old Zen *Koan* (a paradoxical question dedicated to awakening the student by making him or her think outside the box), "What comes first – the chicken or the egg?" Sooner or later, they came to the realization that something must have changed within them to dream me up differently… Of course, I knew all along that I had to change first.

Holding Out pattern of tension

Back in the 90's, Carlos Castaneda once asked me whom I would like to see as my students. I answered that I would like to coach people who have something in common with me, be that a natural curiosity, an open, yet skeptical mind, enthusiasm for all kinds of adventures, or pursuit of authentic mastery in Qigong without any mumbo-jumbo. Lo and behold, my dream came true and I manifested the students who, unbeknownst to themselves, taught me a lesson about my own holding pattern.

Following its unique logic (some might call it "crazy wisdom") **Qi Dao emphasizes the necessity to learn whatever you can learn from all your holding patterns before being able to transcend them**. It is similar to attending a class that you have not been able to learn anything from. If you keep flunking the same test, you will have to take that class over and over again until you really learn whatever you have to learn there. Only then will you be able to move on with your life-long education. It does not mean that your lessons will become any easier, but at least, you will not be stuck with this one for the rest of your life.

Realm of Consciousness

Holding Out corresponds to a state of mind that may be generous and, at the same time, skeptical or even cynical: "I'd rather hold out for something better." Visualize a typical teenager striving to be cool and accepted, yet rebellious at the same time. What posture do you think best represents this mental attitude? As soon as you assume a "cool" stance you may feel more approachable yet skeptical or even somewhat defiant. In many cultures throughout the world, the body language expressing this attitude would consist of shifting more weight on one foot and cocking the head to the opposite side. Guess how your energy field would need to morph to produce such a holding pattern?

Postural Characteristics

To experience Holding Out pattern of tension, take a Natural Stance and then shift more weight on your left foot. Your weight bearing leg will have to work harder than the other leg, developing tension in the left hip flexors, thighs and calves. With your left hip hiking up, you will have more tension in the muscles on your left side (*obliques* and *quadratus lumborum* muscle, commonly referred to as *QL*). Tilting of your upper body to the left will raise your right shoulder and, most likely, make your head tilt to the right. That will produce tension in the muscles on the left side of your neck (*trapezius* and *scalenes*). Some of my students wondered why tension appears on the left side of the neck while the shortened muscles are the ones on the right. My answer is very simple: although there may be a sort of competition between the muscles on both sides of the neck, once the muscles on the left side have won and the head is tilted to the left, the muscles on the right side have to support the weight of the head.

If you hold this posture long enough, you will feel as though you are developing *scoliosis*, which may be considered a solidified Holding Out pattern. Besides the tension in the weight-bearing leg, you will likely feel some extra tension in the *gluteus*, *piriformis* and the muscle with a funny name *tensor fasciae latae* (usually abbreviated as *TFL*) of the opposite leg, which sometimes compresses the *sciatic nerve,* causing *sciatica* (discomfort or pain shooting down the leg). External rotation of that knee can often cause tension on the medial side of the lower leg due to carrying more weight on the outer edge of that foot. It may be happening to the weight bearing foot too, which you can easily detect by checking the soles of your shoes. Those who hold themselves in this pattern wear the outer edges of their shoes noticeably more than the inner edges.

Exploring Holding Out

A chronic shift of your weight to your left can enable you to perform an Opening with the left arm very easily, because your energy field is already morphed sideways. If you shift your weight to the right, you will find it quite easy to make an Opening with the right arm.

You will probably find it still possible to make other directional movements while Holding Out, but not as effortlessly as an Opening on the weight bearing side. Making a Closing may turn out to be exceedingly difficult though, especially with the arm on the weight-bearing side. Qi Dao does not recommend fighting against the energy flow, but rather allowing yourself to learn as much as you can about being on the edge of your comfort zone. Instead of forcing your energy field to morph back to the center, allow it to expand in all directions using all the other directional movements thereby making you more Centered and energetically balanced.

Holding Down

If you find yourself habitually Holding Down, it may often feel as if someone else is holding you down. You may feel put upon, oppressed, or even humiliated by others. This usually means that you do not feel in charge of your life, projecting the sense of not having power over your own experiences. If you think that you are "not good enough," you may also be giving others power over you.

Holding Down often appears as a *somatic* manifestation of depression. Like all the other patterns of holding tension, Holding Down is often coupled with a number of symptoms ranging from pain in the neck to stomach ache and *angina* (chest pain). These can be attributed to the energy blockages resulting from tension in the associated muscle groups responsible for energy deficiency or stagnation in the related areas of the physical body.

Holding Down pattern of tension

Since the practice of Qi Dao does not involve diagnosis and treatment of any symptoms, the objective of your current studies is exploration of the learning opportunities presented by holding patterns. **Recognizing the wisdom of the flow of your life will teach you to trust that it always guides you in the exact direction you need to explore.** You will really benefit from your journey of discovery as soon as you learn to appreciate your current experiences. Holding Down may add some extra challenge to this trip by making you feel less confident. Rest assured, the more experiences you allow yourself to have, the more experienced you will become and the more confidence you will find in yourself.

I suspect that if some wise man advised you that you should just stop being so depressed all the time and become more self-confident, such admonitions would lead nowhere. During the years of coaching hundreds of people, I noticed that nobody seemed to be able to follow through with my choices and decisions regarding their behavior or character. Yet most people proved to be quite capable of following through with those decisions and choices they made for themselves. Therefore, I simply invite you to explore your holding patterns until you clearly feel an internal motivation and inner guidance to change. **Since change is the most constant thing in the Universe, the most harmonious way to deal with it is being in the flow of change.**

Realm of Consciousness

It is usually pretty easy to point out the traits of a person chronically Holding Down: low self-esteem, humble, depressed, ashamed, etc. It is not all negative though, because those who experience this Holding Pattern on a regular basis unconsciously use it as their survival mechanism, which allows them to cope with the challenges of life. You, too, can experience it by invoking the corresponding state of mind if you keep telling yourself and others, "I'm not good enough."

If you keep Holding Down long enough, you may even become aware of another peculiar quality associated with this holding pattern – seeking love and sympathy from others in an unconscious hope to prove that you are "good enough." For most people, even in the depths of self-pity, there is still some hope. Qi Dao philosophy of life does not propose holding onto any hope, but rather teaches you to go through the challenging phase of life without wishing that it were not happening. To paraphrase Winston Churchill, **when going through hell – keep on going – you do not have to be stuck there!**

Postural Characteristics

You can experiment with the Holding Down pattern of tension by contracting your abdomen, which will pull your sternum down, making your shoulders slouch and your head hang down. Inevitably, your back will round, decreasing the lumbar curve causing the condition called *kyphosis* whereby the whole body assumes the shape of a question mark. This will eventually result in a noticeable amount of tension in the *erector spinae* and other muscles of the back and neck. It is as if the muscle groups of the front of your body were competing against the ones on your back, where the muscles of the front overpowered the back muscles and now the latter have to support the weight of the upper torso. Without holding that tension, your body would simply collapse.

Since your *abdominals* pull the sternum and pubic bone closer together, your pelvis tilts backwards while the knees bend slightly. Tension in *biceps femoris* (hamstrings) has to coexist with and counter-balance tension in *rectus femoris* (thigh muscles). Unlike most other patterns of holding tension, Holding Down allows for being Grounded, which entails distributing your weight on the centers of the feet. Yet there is another major challenge associated with this pattern – it is quite hard to breathe when the *abs* are constantly short, which continuously compresses the *diaphragm* and restricts its movement.

Exploring Holding Down

While you are Holding Down, experiment with your ability to project energy in that direction using Downward Press. You may notice that as long as your entire energy field keeps morphing down, Downward Press is relatively easy to execute whereas Upper Cut becomes almost impossible to perform. If you are one of those who habitually hold themselves down, enjoy practicing Downward Press, which will eventually bring you right to the edge of your comfort zone. Perhaps, it will even make you really mad at yourself for allowing everything and everyone to put you down, which means you are ready to realize the true meaning of this holding pattern. As soon as you integrate it into your expanded awareness, you will be able to enjoy the freedom to move in any direction equally gracefully. Exploring other directional movements will harmonize this particular flow of energy with your entire energy field and will empower you to actualize your full potential.

Holding Up

If you happen to routinely experience this holding pattern, you may consciously understand that self-importance does not make anyone happier but still continue Holding Up unconsciously as a matter of habit. Holding Up pattern generally reflects the sense of superiority and self-importance. Some people may temporarily experience it when they feel proud of themselves or contemptuous. Others may serve you as constant reminders that arrogance and narcissism are among the main reasons people tend to get energetically stuck in the head.

Holding Up pattern of tension

I doubt that there is any panacea that could cure this condition once and for all, since **enlightenment, which can be understood as freedom from ego, is not a state but a process**. Qi Dao offers you some methods that allow shifting from one way of being to another without fighting against the old pattern. If it used to serve you as your survival mechanism, who knows when it may came in handy once again? Integrating all potentially usable aspects of your being can be done without developing your identity on the basis of the beliefs forming any rigid pattern of holding tension.

If Holding Up is really ingrained into your sense of self, shifting out of this pattern of holding tension may feel threatening to the very existence of the personality you identify with. Nothing is more threatening to the ego than the realization that it is nothing but a bunch of empty phrases and stories without any real substance. As the word "persona" originates from the masks that ancient Greek actors wore on stage, I consider the ego to consist of two layers: the inner layer is your identity that constitutes the sum total of your beliefs and attitudes you identify with; the outer layer is your personality that you present to others hoping to receive their acceptance and attention. Both are two sides of the same coin, as it were, influencing and interfering with each other at the same time.

My philosophical paradigm suggests that the patterns of ego dynamics and internal conflicts can be perceived as the interference between these two images forming a hologram that you recreate moment by moment. **Indeed, your ego is a pure figment of your imagination, a dream character in quest of lucidity**. A consistent practice of reminding yourself and your practice partner(s) about the dream-like nature of existence is the most direct way to facilitate mutual spiritual awakening.

Realm of Consciousness

You can experiment with morphing your energy field upward by imagining yourself more important than others around you. I believe that self-importance is usually established through social interactions rather than natural instincts and senses. Can you imagine anyone interacting this way with a wild animal or a bird? Just imagine yourself Holding Up to a squirrel, thinking, "I'm more important than you!" Only when dealing with other humans may you feel the need to demonstrate superiority.

This sense of self-importance is often coupled with self-doubt, since there would be no reason for anyone to prove their power if they were totally sure about it. On the other hand, the very fact that this pattern of holding tension is sustained means that the full expression of the emotions associated with it is restricted (as you may remember, tension is frozen movement), revealing some degree of non-acceptance of these emotions in one's mind. In other words, one's current way of being does not match the dream of being somehow greater in one way or another.

Postural Characteristics

The term *lordosis* comes from the observation of the postural characteristics particularly apparent among nobility. To experience the Holding Up pattern of tension, try to emulate a proud British Lord. Pull your chin up, shoulders down, lock your knees and increase the *lumbar* curve of your spine at the waist level. If you pay attention to the muscles you need to contract in order to create such changes in your body, you will notice tension in the back of the neck, under your shoulder blades, lower back, and *hip flexors*. This combination of tension can easily contribute to *lordosis*, also known as sway back – misalignment of the spine often responsible for lower back pain.

Another peculiar experience specific to Holding Up is tension in the *ilio-costalis* muscles participating in pulling the shoulders down. As their Latin name implies, these muscles connect the pelvis with the ribs. Although not reaching all the way to the shoulders, they are still involved in compensatory tension required for increasing the distance between the head and shoulders.

In addition to that, tension in the *quadriceps* usually causes overextension and locking of the knee joints when standing or even walking. If you try making a few steps while keeping your legs straight, you will experience a fair amount of shock in the joints of the knees, hips and throughout the entire length of the spine. If you constantly hurt all these joints with each and every step you take on earth, it would bring about various pains and aches usually blamed on such ailments as *rheumatoid arthritis*.

Exploring Holding Up

The energy field of a person Holding Up morphs upwards. That makes it relatively easy to perform any movement in that direction, like an Upper Cut, but movements requiring bending the knees, like Downward Press, become awkward and difficult. In fact, if you try to perform Downward Press while Holding Up, you will probably experience tension and/or pain in your lower back, because of bending over instead of bending the knees.

If you are one of those who dream of grandeur, you can become lucid in this dream by using Upper Cut to shift your energy field even further upwards until you reach the edge of your comfort zone. Be careful not to push yourself beyond that edge (you may feel dizzy or lightheaded) but just feel the flow of changes once you are on the edge. With some observation, you may notice that the ever-changing flow of *Qi* begins to guide you in some other direction. You may express your readiness to be in the flow by altering your movements to match the new direction, which is also subject to change.

The flow always continues to flow even if you think you are stuck or blocked from reaching your innermost dreams. Allowing your perspective to change accordingly will eventually enlighten you as to the lessons you can learn from this holding pattern. More over, this newly discovered fluidity of your perspective on yourself and your world may remind you of being in a dream where dream characters and dreamscapes tend to morph and transform spontaneously. Once you become lucid, you may even realize that **you can dream yourself up as a Centered person who is free to be in the flow of energy going in any direction**.

Transcending Holding Patterns

To excel in transcending your holding patterns, you would ideally receive Qi Dao Coaching from me or another certified Qi Dao Coach capable of utilizing some advanced practices beyond the scope of this basic book. During my studies of Hypnotherapy, I found out that certain aspects of Qi Dao Coaching are comparable to what Dr. Ernest Rossi considered "the Symptom Path to Enlightenment." It really leads to enlightenment or, at least, fulfillment of your greatest dreams as well as empowering you to assist others in their self-realization. Initially starting with a series of therapeutic sessions, it could eventually develop into learning how to coach others to actualize their hidden potentials. That would provide you with plenty of opportunities to see lessons behind any challenges and idiosyncrasies. You may discover for yourself that coaching is also a mutually beneficial process, since **the more people you assist in manifesting their dreams the more people will help you in manifesting yours**.

To receive a first-hand experience with Qi Dao Coaching, please visit www.qidao.org/coaching and enroll into my coaching program. At the commencement of our coaching relationship, I would like to establish a reasonable degree of rapport with you by being fully present and open to your interpretations of your experiences. I have no real need for your medical history and would not ask you to retell me those stories that make you think "This is who I have always been – it is the story of my life" and thereby habituating the memories and traumas lingering in your body-mind. Your past experiences leave their imprints on you for as long as you keep identifying with the same old beliefs and attitudes perpetuated by those stories and letting their energies run your life. Since I can do only so much to change your past, my attention is typically focused on the present energetic conditions that you have to deal with as well as the dreams you strive to manifest.

Qi Dao Coaching often begins with learning that holding patterns represent archetypal emotional, psychological, spiritual and energetic perspectives. Not only the movements of your body (both manifest and unmanifest) constantly express your consciousness; your habitual physical postures also reveal imbalances of your energy field when you are not Centered. Struggling against the energetic imbalances can really feel like a nightmare – the more you struggle, the more you suffer. **Although tension and pain are natural responses of the organism to energetic imbalances, suffering is optional**; it depends on your choice whether to maintain the gap between the present and the future, onto which you can project the feelings about your pain.

If you opt to continue suffering, all you need to do is to polarize the present and your dream by choosing one over the other and telling yourself and others: "This is the way I will always be" or "I wish I were like this, but I know I am not!" On the other hand, if you opt to relinquish suffering, consider surrendering your old ways of thinking and allowing a new, integrated state of consciousness to emerge. The process of integration is similar to the process of creating synthesis out of thesis and antithesis that allows unifying these seemingly opposing perspectives without the old contradictions.

One of the most direct ways to deal with suffering is through addressing any discrepancies between your current state of affairs (although it is a process rather than a state) and whatever dreams you aspire to manifest. If there is a gap between your present and dream states, it is understandable that you may be inclined to reject the present, since the dream is more compelling to experience than whatever is happening here and now. You may dream of having a better partner, house or job; you may dream of feeling better about yourself or your life; you may ultimately aspire to become the person you have always dreamt of being – wiser, stronger or somehow better than you are now.

Whatever you are daydreaming about, you can use this process to learn to be as awake in your daydreams, as you can be in a lucid night dream. Since all holding patterns are essentially unconscious strategies distracting you from being present with emotional and physical pain, they will no longer need to exist when there is no difference between your dreams and the present moment. When you live your dreams, you no longer need to hold yourself in any way (unless you consciously choose to play some witty role in your dream drama, which thereby magically transforms into a comedy).

I often begin coaching by asking some straightforward questions: "What would you like to experience as the most desirable result of your sessions?" and "How will you know that you have manifested that dream?" or "How would you need to be in order for this dream to come true?" You probably know how infrequently people focus on what they want to manifest but constantly worry about whatever they do not want. Obviously, it is much easier to manifest your dreams when you know exactly what they are. Your ability to answer these kinds of questions means that you have the corresponding energy within your system that is capable of creating such visions and making them vivid, almost tangible. You may even imagine smelling or tasting things in your dreams, which can, in turn, increase their clarity and realism. Although I may give you some time to enjoy your daydreaming, I am not necessarily interested in the details of your imagery and would rather focus your attention on the energy that you embody in your dreams (of course, you are made of energy in your dream just like every other dream character).

As you work on perceiving your dream energy, I would invite you to take a Natural Stance and extend both hands in front of you to check which hand might feel greater resonance with this type of energy. Once you have identified the hand detecting any peculiar feelings of heat, weight, tingling, itchiness or other sensations indicating greater resonance with this particular energy, I would suggest gathering this energy field on the palm as if it were an air balloon or energy ball. It may take some practice and perseverance, but by now you know that it is entirely worth your time to concentrate on your dream energy. As an alternative, you may visualize a little figure that represents you being the way you strive to be standing on the palm of that hand surrounded with the energy field corresponding to the state of consciousness required for manifesting your dream.

The second step is to return to the present and imagine perceiving yourself the way you are at the moment from a third party's perspective. Without paying too much attention to the details of your appearance, you can just visualize your current energy field associated with your *psychosomatic* conditions as well as your current beliefs and state of consciousness. As with the dream energy, you may just imagine a small figure representing you as you are at the present moment standing on the palm of the other hand surrounded by the aura of matching energy.

As you gather the energy field related to your current state of affairs on the palm of that hand, you create a unique situation, in which you invoke both states of being and their corresponding energies. I usually do not need to tell you what to do with those energy fields you are holding in your hands. All I might suggest is to let them communicate and exchange with each other whatever they have to share or need to learn from each other. I often prefer to present this suggestion in a form of a question: "What would happen if you allowed these two energy fields to communicate with each other?" If you do not notice anything happening for a while, I might ask, "Isn't it interesting, how your hands can be magnetized by this energy to remain so still until they begin to move, which is also an indication that you are ready to experience some transformation?"

As the next step in this process, one or both parts of your consciousness may take advantage of this opportunity to express themselves through voice, movement or other means. This would allow your formerly disconnected or dissociated parts of the *psyche* to reveal their values, desires, or grievances, thus transforming your tensions into manifest movements. If some active movements arise, I might encourage further exploration by asking you something to the effect of: "Aren't you curious to find out where these movements would take you?" or "Fascinating how your inner nature can take charge of the healing process, is it not?"

My questions are designed to foster your curiosity and ease any doubts as to the reality of these spontaneous movements and simultaneous changes in your consciousness. As you recognize in the privacy of your body-mind that the formerly polarized or even conflicting energies begin to organize themselves into a unified field of energy, some revelations may come to mind, some hidden memories may surface and become integrated, as well as some spiritual insights may enlighten you. Indeed, once you surrender to the flow of Qi, you no longer exercise the will of the ego, or your known self, which is just the tip of the iceberg of your being. The greater part of you comes into play – the deep, unknown part of the iceberg that is also the deep part of each and every one of us. Allowing this unknown and unmanifest aspect of reality to emerge is akin to allowing whatever is about to become manifest to see the light of day. It is not even that you let manifestation happen, for the only thing you can do about it, other than struggle against it, is to surrender to the process of manifestation and go with its flow.

The final part of this process of integration entails bringing the unified field of *Qi* into your organism to empower whatever needs to be empowered in order to have the capacity to continue this journey. It will likely boost and alter your *psyche*, aligning it with the Dream Being. Enjoy bringing the energy ball into various parts of your body-mind and observe Qi flowing wherever it needs to flow to empower every one of the cells, organs and systems of your organism. You may notice some gradual or, sometime, radical changes in the way you hold yourself as well as in many other aspects of your life.

Closing the gap between the way you are at the present moment and the way you need to be to manifest your dreams can seriously enhance the quality of your life. With practice, you will discover a greater sense of equanimity, which is identical to being Centered, thus preventing stress from building to the levels harmful to your health and well-being. The practice of Qi Dao will empower you to shift in and out of various states of consciousness required for one type of activity or another, while still maintaining the ability to freely return to your Neutral state. Being Centered will also help you develop a greater sensitivity to the subtle flows of energy within and around your body, since you will no longer struggle with the constant pull of your energy field off Center that can throw you off balance. This will build a strong foundation for mastering being in the flow.

Conclusion

More advanced practices of Qi Dao are primarily based on learning to perceive the flow of energy and surrendering to it, trusting that **the flow always takes you exactly where you need to go in order to experience whatever you are supposed to experience**. Once you have been initiated into the practice of Empowerment, you will learn to enter an amazing state of consciousness, aptly called Qigong state. It will empower you to manifest your dreams simply by being in the flow of the dream called life and experiencing oneness with Dream Being.

How can you be one with Dream Being, traditionally referred to as the Dao? To answer this question, let's take another look at who you are and what your mode of being is at the present moment. It would not be too great of an exaggeration to say that most people have a culturally programmed frame of mind, which helps them keep their attention focused on particular things in their lives that they deem especially important. Yet, what is utterly important to one person may be irrelevant to another, or even ridiculously unimportant to others. How often do people experience misunderstandings concerning the most basic things or ideas such as money issues, family relationships, religious beliefs, etc.?

Metaphorically speaking, humankind can be viewed as an island in the ocean of life with a number of villages located on different sides of the island. The islanders in each village have historically developed a tradition of building their houses in a particular direction. It may simply be the direction towards the ocean, which varies depending on the side of the island. If you were born and raised in one of the villages on this island, then you were most likely taught from a very early age that, when you grow up, you should build your house facing the specific direction customary to your native village. You would be thoroughly indoctrinated to make sure your identity, beliefs and worldviews were aligned with the conventional views of your village.

People living on different sides of the island may, at times, try to communicate with each other, but most of their communication only causes more trouble because of the profound dissimilarities between the perspectives specific to different villages. Due to their beliefs about the importance of their own "right" direction, villagers on one side of the island often consider the inhabitants of other sides strange, to say the least. They may even believe that the people on the opposite side of the island are totally wrong in their worldviews, if not downright evil.

Miscommunication and differences in viewpoints cause most of human conflicts and wars. Many of us also assume that the grass on the other side of the island is greener than on our own side. Consequently, the feelings of greed, envy and unrest arise. Have you ever tried to improve your life by leaving your old home, work, or partner, hoping that the new one would make you happier? How can you sit here quietly when someone over there seems to enjoy a better life than you?! But when it comes to being truly where the grass is supposed to be greener, you may suddenly feel anxious about getting into an unexplored territory (perhaps, having to oust the former inhabitant of the place) just to realize that you may continue feeling dissatisfied, wanting again juicier grass, more grass, more possessions, hoping to satisfy the never-ending list of human desires. Such a state of discontentment may be very frustrating, invoking suffering as well as cruelty towards others. This state is usually based on the belief (perhaps an unconscious projection) suggesting that other people are selfish and competitive, which results in constant stress.

Spiritual implications of adhering to this selfish perspective are quite profound: **your realm of existence depends on the particular position you occupy on our island**, which manifests *somatically* as a holding pattern. Everything you perceive with such tunnel vision is polarized on the scale of importance from the most important things in life that are the closest to you to the least important things that are farther away in this one-dimensional perspective. You may feel that your honor, title, money, property, family, country, or whatever, is more important than anyone else's identity, possessions or beliefs. To many islanders, their worldviews are the most important item, for their belief systems intrinsically connect them with the places on the island they occupy. We all know of innumerable cases of people risking or even sacrificing their lives (or the lives of others) due to their attachment to their beliefs.

If you show any disloyalty, there is also a threat that you may get exiled for your lack of allegiance to the social consensus or chased out of your old village. You will then have an option to perceive this as a huge problem or as an awesome learning opportunity. You may choose to wander around the island learning about other villages with their perspectives and corresponding realms of consciousness. Potential for adventures abounds, because other sides of the island represent alternative realms of human existence, some of them totally condemned and cursed by certain islanders. It appears as though the inhabitants of the East side of the island consider the West side to be an abode of evil forces, while the Westerners think the same about those from the East.

As you become more and more familiar with various realms around the island, you may eventually come to a realization that none of them is more or less important than any other. Neither perspective offers the complete view of reality, but together they form a wider field of vision eventually opening up to 360 degrees. If you continue your walkabout around the island long enough, you will inevitably discover a large lagoon in the center of the island. It has always been there, but you habitually kept your attention fixed on the dry land, which represents the element of Earth. This fixation exists mainly due to the way **the human mind prefers to pay attention to things that have a form and can be given a name**. Waves and swells in the lagoon have no particular form and cannot be easily labeled; besides, the fact that they are in constant ebb and flow makes it difficult to fixate attention on them. Most islanders, whose houses face away from the center of their island, are not even aware that the lagoon is there.

Eventually, most adventurers who stumble upon the lagoon get curious to test the water in it. Moving in water feels so different from walking on dry land, yet it is a lot of fun! Those who tried it once will never be the same, for their minds and bodies discovered another element of nature – the element of Water. It is certainly safer to learn swimming inside the lagoon protected by the island from the oceanic currents, tides and surf. The more experiences you have in swimming and frolicking in water, the more experienced you will be in utilizing this elemental energy.

Ordinary human awareness of energy is like the tip of an iceberg – most people are consciously aware of only a little tip sticking above the surface of the water. Over 90% of human energy potential is still a mystery to most of us. As the submerged part of the iceberg, which is frozen water, constantly melts, transforming into the element of Water, the human mind can melt and become fluid, too. It happens totally naturally to every one of us when we relax and let go of mental and physical tensions; you may feel like meditating or just daydreaming. It is when the mode of being prevails over the mode of doing or having something.

Many mystical traditions venerate such a spontaneous meditation as a blissful way of *Wu Wei* (non-doing) that leads nowhere but to your own inner essence, your true nature. The practice of Empowerment is particularly suited to help you switch from striving to reach some mythical spiritual destination to truly enjoying the journey. As in surfing, this spiritual journey is not about getting from point A to point B but rather about enjoying being in the flow moment by moment. When you shift your attention from the one-dimensional realm of the element of Earth to the two-dimensional world of the element of Water, you will find yourself enjoying a new, effortless and spontaneous culture of movement. At the same time, you will discover that your mind gets quieter, no longer judging and labeling things the way it used to.

From the one-dimensional reality of the strip of land surrounding the lagoon, you can step into the two-dimensional water world in the center of the island. It is not better or worse there, it is completely different. Another degree of freedom allows you to circumvent direct confrontations with most fellow humans habitually operating on the energy of the element of Earth. What can they do to you? They may try to push your buttons or attack with their full force while you remain calm and Centered redirecting their attacks and utilizing their own forcefulness to teach them a lesson. Any assailant operating on energy of the element of Earth in his attempt to prove his superiority to you would resemble a samurai swinging his sword against the river. He can hack water to his heart's content, but only until a particularly strong wave picks him up and gives him a lesson in going with the flow.

Speaking of the flow, surfing offers a different, more enticing example of being in the flow. Catching a wave requires perceptivity and great timing. You need to observe a lot of waves to figure out when and where to attempt to ride one. You've got to be right on time, neither too early nor too late to catch your wave; and if you paddle too fast or too slow, it will be impossible for you to ride it. We will delve into the subject of timing in our advanced books; I will just mention here that timing is as crucial for a Qi Dao practitioner as it is for a surfer.

Although the lagoon is a great place to learn about the element of Water, to catch really big waves you need to go into the open sea. There you'll be able to learn navigation and even discover other islands in the limitless ocean of life. While the lagoon symbolizes trance and meditative states of mind, the ocean represents dreaming. The waves of dreams wash the shores of our island every night, as well as during the day, bringing the news from the unknown and delivering messages from other lands. When you dream, you also become like a wave roaming the ocean of Dream Being. You may feel as though you have a separate identity, but to perceive a wave as an independent entity would be delusional. **We are all interconnected dream beings – facets of the universal Dream Being – just as waves are inseparable from the ocean.**

Some people more frequently than others get a chance to be jolted awake enough to recognize that they are dreaming when they have nightmares or encounter some monsters in their dreams. Different dreamers have different attitudes towards their dream dramas, but at least once in a blue moon anyone can experience moments of lucidity or conscious dreaming. Then you can realize that you are dreaming at the present moment and the entire dream world with all its inhabitants is dreamed up by you. You may even realize that your dream characters are projections of your own consciousness representing different aspects of it during the Dreamtime. They are not separate from you but totally interdependent and interconnected by the means of energy fields that may even be visible to the dreamer's eye. The power of *Qi* manifests through the interplay of these energy fields and channels animating the entire dream world and every creature in it.

In more advanced Qi Dao books, I will return to the subject of lucid dreaming to explore it in-depth. You will see that there is no end to the adventures in the third dimension, starting with a huge new area for exploration – the underworld. It is the realm forbidden to the ordinary islanders, where only Shamans and mythical heroes go when undertaking their epic quests for knowledge and power. That is where you will discover and hone the skills and powers of the element of Air. That is right; paradoxically, you can begin exploring that new realm by submerging yourself underwater in order to learn how to move in three-dimensional space. Observing the way most islanders relate to the ocean, you may notice that they never dive underwater but just cast their fishing lines and nets into the water and then wait to see what is going to come up – the catch of the day, as they say, or of the night rather, since this is an obvious metaphor for dreaming.

Who knows what might come up from the depths of the unconscious? You never know what dreams may come. As you begin exploring the underwater world, you immerse yourself in a completely different reality under the surface of the ocean that remains unknown until you immerse yourself in it. As you explore the underworld, you will likely encounter different creatures that inhabit that world, completely different from those creatures that live on dry land. They may not even need to breathe air; most of them can breathe water and move in a totally unique fashion.

Through the practice of Dream Yoga, a major component of Qi Dao, you will also be able to learn that manipulating the flow of dreaming is similar to trying to manipulate the whole universe; therefore, the best thing you can do about it is to surrender to the power of the Dream Being that is much greater than your personal power. This surrender is metaphorically synonymous to the process of boiling water and evaporating it into steam. Like any kind of gas, it symbolizes a distinct element – the element of Air. This element has such unique qualities as being able to compress and expand, being invisible while capable of influencing hard matter and fluids, and being as incredibly free as wind. In the case of the human body, the most vivid example of the work of air is breathing. Visualize the flow of air circulating in and out of your lungs during breathing – throughout your entire life. There is really no distinction between the air inside of you and the air outside; this elemental force flows freely within as well as without. You can compare this with air that is the same above the island and above the ocean. **When you wake up to the true nature of reality in your dream, you may also come to the realization of sameness of your dream-being with the totality of the dream-world**.

The longer you explore the underworld the more you will grow curious about another way to explore the third dimension – exploring three-dimensional space through flight. Indeed, you will also learn how to take off and fly (metaphorically, of course, unless you are dreaming). These practices of the element of Air will allow you to experience new ways of perception. It is like being able to see the big picture instead of seeing just what is immediately in front of your nose when you are under water. From this bird's eye point of view, you will be able to see the whole island of humankind at once. Believe it or not, you will also be able to fly to visit some other islands that represent different sentient beings.

No worries, you will be able to come back to regain your human shape and frame of mind, but you will no longer have to be stuck on this little island. Feeling slightly detached from the activities and affairs of its denizens is similar to being in this world but not of this world at the same time. You will also learn an alternative way to deal with obstacles in your path: Those operating on the energy of the element of Earth usually act as if they believe that when they run into an obstacle they have to choose from either banging their head against it trying to break through, or withdraw and run away. This is a "fight or flight" reaction that we have discussed earlier in this book.

When you shift into the element of Water, you may start acting like water. When you run into an obstacle, you continue to flow. Water will find its way around the barrier somewhere, somehow. You may not know where or how, but as you keep flowing, you will eventually travel around the obstacle, which will no longer have to be perceived as such. It will become a landmark that happened to be on the side of your path rather than blocking it. This usually coincides with starting to perceive such situations as learning opportunities rather than problems.

As you continue exploring the element of Air, you will learn to fly over any obstacles in addition to flowing around them. You can accomplish this by shifting from one level of awareness to another. You may begin applying this enlightened attitude when you find yourself running against some obstacles on your runway, such as your own island. When you get into the flow while exploring the lagoon at the center of the island, you may perceive the land as an obstacle in your way, but instead of crushing into it you may fly over it. It is a matter of your perspective on things – you either perceive them as roadblocks in your way destined to stop your movement, or you accept them as challenges destined to make you overcome them by going higher.

By changing the frequencies of the universal energy that you identify with, you can change everything in your world. The bird's eye point of view will allow you to perceive everything on your island as well as on the surface of the sea from a totally new perspective, seeing yourself and other people much more objectively. You will be able to see from the new perspective that your obstacles are actually intrinsic aspects of the flow of things in your life. They may even help you with navigating when flying around and enjoying the great freedom of the element of Air. Of course, new obstacles may appear, but the old ones will usually remain on their respective planes. This does not mean that you will never have to deal with any challenges, but you will have learned how to shift to other planes of existence in a timely fashion.

After mastering the element of Air, you will be able to explore navigating in the fourth dimension, the dimension of time, the realm of the element of Fire. Synchronicity will eventually become your ultimate feedback device, your interface with the fourth dimension. The ability to modulate your perception of time is a prerequisite for becoming a real Qi Dao master. Learning to perceive time in alternative ways will eventually transform your practice of energy arts into bona fide sorcery.

The Dreamtime is obviously different from the linear time that most of us are used to in the civilized world. The linear or mechanical time is constantly measured with the use of timepieces that people check when they want to know the time. According to many Shamanic traditions, the flow of time has much more to do with the flow of dreaming than with any mechanical devices, for the Dreamtime does not flow from the past straight into the future. Instead, it has a certain nonlinear, sometimes spiral, or even spherical, flow to it. It may be perceived as enveloping and encompassing each and every moment, always being the present moment whenever you check it. **Any time you look at your Dreamtime clock, it shows the same time – the Dreamtime**.

Knowing that you are in the Dreamtime will serve you as a constant reminder that you are dreaming, thereby enabling you to be consistently lucid. With enough practice, you will be able to realize that you are the dreamer and identify with the Dream Being instead of perceiving it as something or someone separate that is doing things to you in your dreams. With the help of the element of Fire practices, you will learn to translate this sense of lucidity into your daily life, too. What I call enlightenment is being completely lucid and awake to the reality of the dream called life. The Dream Being, the creator of this dream, resides within you, as well as within each and every one of us – it is our true nature. As soon as you realize this, you will be able to identify with the creator of your life as well as the entire creation, including each and every dream character in this magical universe that is dreaming itself into existence.

Please keep in mind that the decision to engage in the practices associated with the element of Fire cannot be made by your ego, because it would threaten the very existence of the ego by exposing what it really is – a bunch of stories that attempt to label and control mystery that exists beyond time. For some mystical reason, you manifested in this world as a human being, the Dream Being having an experience of living a human life. Now you are learning not only to remember who you really are, but also to enlighten the entire universe by becoming spiritually awake and realizing oneness with the Dao.

Does this reveal the meaning of life? Maybe… you can experience your own revelation as to the meaning and purpose of your life. As for me, **balancing the bewilderment of being a human being with the miracle of being the Dream Being is a mighty fine reason for practicing this magical art called Qi Dao**.

About the Author

Lama Somananda Tantrapa is the holder of the lineage of Qi Dao that has been fostered in his clan for 27 generations since 1224 AD. He has over 30 years of experience in Qi Dao and other internal martial arts. He was primarily trained by his Grandfather who was the last Grand Master of this style of Tibetan Shamanic Qigong. In addition to being recognized as an incarnate Bön lama, ordained as a Buddhist monk and initiated into Subud spiritual brotherhood, Rinpoche holds a degree in Cultural Anthropology and certifications in Qigong, Hypnosis and NLP.

Affectionately addressed by his students as Rinpoche, Lama Tantrapa's initiatives dedicated to peace work and spiritual freedom were subjected to persecution in his homeland thus he received religious asylum in the United States in 1997. His unique background is complex enough to include serving in the Soviet Army's Special Forces, being kidnapped in the Ukraine and going through several near-death experiences.

Rinpoche's coaching has inspired many professional athletes, speakers, dancers, singers, writers and actors to open up to the infinite source of intuition that exists within everyone. After founding Academy of Qi Dao – the first and only school specifically dedicated to Tibetan Shamanic Qigong Coaching – in 2000, he has provided peak performance, enlightenment and life coaching to hundreds of clients of all ages from all walks of life.

Rinpoche is the author of numerous articles as well as multimedia training materials. Being an avid speaker and presenter, he has appeared on many radio and TV programs in the US, Guam and abroad. He currently serves on the Board of Directors of the USA National Qigong (Chi Kung) Association.

For more information about Qi Dao Coaching, workshops, retreats, and long-distance learning opportunities, feel free to request a complimentary introduction with Rinpoche or one of his apprentices at www.qidao.org/intro.

About the Companion DVD

Qi Dao DVD, designed as a companion for this ground-breaking book, takes you on a journey of discovering a greater sense of aliveness. Step-by-step, you will explore the process of self-realization using this unique system of energy work dedicated to helping you discover and harness the inner powers dormant in most people. This ancient art of awareness can be applied to virtually any sphere of life: from healing to martial arts and from workplace to enlightenment!

You must see Lama Tantrapa demonstrating the effortless power that can be achieved by putting just a few of these fundamental principles into practice. He is one of the few Qigong masters throughout the world who can both demonstrate the feats of power most people only dream of and teach you how to develop such mastery. With a regular Qi Dao practice, you will learn how to:

- Manage and prevent stress
- Free yourself from tension and pain
- Increase your flexibility and range of motion
- Improve your balance with kinesthetic awareness training
- Develop the Harmonious Culture of Movement specific to Qi Dao
- Learn to send energy waves through your body and project *Qi*
- Become more centered, grounded, attentive and present
- Experience self-realization and spiritual awakening.

Purchase this DVD online at www.qidao.org/dvd101.

About the Qi Dao Home Study Course

Discover the magic of Tibetan Dream Yoga as taught by Lama Somananda Tantrapa. In addition to this book, the companion DVD, Qi Dao Initiation CD, as well as the audiobook and workbook, are included into the Qi Dao Home Study Course. You may enjoy the practices presented in this Course on your own, although it is easier to learn and master with a practice partner or a Certified Qi Dao coach. Being able to test and experiment with all the Qi Dao practices is essential for developing greater sensitivity to subtle flows of *Qi*, which will enable you to be in the flow.

When you complete this Home Study Course you will experience:

- Being accepting of and attentive to your life's lessons
- Being present and never stuck in the head
- Being grounded, rooted and centered
- Being relaxed, natural and spontaneous
- Being awake in the dream called your daily life
- Being in the flow, in the right place and at the right time.

In addition to the foundational practices of Dream Yoga and non-dual awareness presented in the book and DVD, this unique Course also includes Qi Dao Initiation CD serving as a preparation for receiving your Initiation into the practice of Empowerment. This special meditation CD will take you on a mystical journey of discovering your inner world, the world of lucid dreaming and spiritual adventure. A number of unadvertised bonus materials that come with this Course will also help you transcend any old, less than optimal beliefs and patterns, so you can become fully aware of who you really are.

Please order the Qi Dao Home Study Course online at www.qidao.org/course101.

Qi Dao Practitioner Certification Program

There is NOTHING like this program anywhere... period. No other system of Qigong and energy arts offers such a full spectrum of skills and applications developed in this tradition by the generations of enlightened masters. The power and sophistication of the Internal Martial Arts unified with the spiritual potential of Yoga and Zen meditation... less the repetitive routines of daily meditation or holding poses. And the best thing about learning Qi Dao is its applicability to virtually any sphere of life: from peacemaking to lovemaking to moneymaking (except mixing the latter two).

The deeper you immerse yourself into the world of Qi Dao, the fuller will be your appreciation of this ancient tradition. Of course, your success is going to depend on your commitment and consistency. It will reflect the degree, to which you choose to enjoy this life-long learning opportunity and are willing to share it with other people to promote their empowerment and enlightenment. If you aspire to become a Certified Qi Dao Practitioner or even a Qi Dao Coach, now you have an opportunity to enroll into Qi Dao Practitioner Certification Program offered by Academy of Qi Dao.

If you are already in our Program, you are in for a real treat! If you are not involved in it yet, but would like to experience Qi Dao Coaching first-hand, feel free to request a complimentary coaching session at www.qidao.org/intro. Receiving coaching sessions from a Certified Qi Dao Coach will rapidly advance the depth of your studies and help you gain a practical understanding of energy work. There is no better way to excel in The Art of Being in the Flow than by learning from the Qi Dao lineage holder and other top experts. Completing this Program may even lead you to receiving an Initiation into the Qi Dao tribe of spiritual adventurers.

To enroll in the program, apply today at www.qidao.org/program101.

CPSIA information can be obtained at www.ICGtesting.com
Printed in the USA
BVOW081049130713

325805BV00001B/160/P

9 781434 320278